v v v

I Am Because We Are

v v v

Preface

Communities are a perfect example of something greater than the sum of its parts. The online poetry community Allpoetry brings together the poets in this book – the "we" helps each of us express our "I."

"It takes a village" is a commonly used phrase about raising children, but it's true in other aspects of life as well – we build upon each other. One person's brilliance helps inspire and lift up the other members. There is less "me" and more "us."

These poems celebrate this sense of community while also be tempered by the individual expression of each poet. I hope you can enjoy and celebrate these poems as much as I have been.

Contents

[Aadil Wahid]

The machines

As I look to the sea
the machines
look back at me,

with searchlights
that flicker like starlight
and smokestacks
belching smog
and steam
holding firm
to the headland
from the encroach
of the green

Yet these giants
of iron
steel
and tin
command not the sands
appease the seas
or sooth wind's rage
against chapped skin

So I watch them
watching me
as the crescent beach
births

new dunes
in wind whipped flurries
that surrender themselves
to the grass hoards
buffering the wind's charge
by the wet lands' edge

And the Curlews
wading in the rippled wash
of tide and mud
continue their dig
for worms
or the prising open
of clam
and muscle,
for not much
is afoot
that is worth
the raising of their heads
or the setting of their plumage
to the wind

———————————

I love the interplay between man's pursuits and nature's almost
ambivalent stance towards it most of the time.
Allpoetry.com/Aadil_Wahid

[S. Libellule]

(I am because we are)

I am because we are
How rare that that may be
A single breath to share
For all Eternity ~

While going hand in hand
Still striding side by side
Across this fertile land
To reach the Ebbing tide.

Dear loving Bride and Groom ~
Oh, how we do unite!
So beautiful our bloom
In darkness or in Light.

Not knowing in the end
How any Story goes ~
Every line meant to blend
While love forever grows.

———————————

Libellule is originally from New England and now lives outside Birmingham, Alabama. The poet writes about nature, authenticity, and the examined life. Influences include Mary Oliver and Billy Collins. Allpoetry.com/Little_Dragonfly

[Brian Peter Hodgkinson]

Wild Child

I was a wild little elf child
romping on eight acres of land
lake and forest
my elvin-eyes filled with magic

the owner of an idyllic childhood home
named Cherry Brook
in the late 1950s
dad and mom built up
a house refurbished
from a dilapidated 1800s barn
situated on
eight acres of untamed sugar-bush forests
with old wagon trails crisscrossing the woods
hung with grapevines

dad also dredged a lake and built a dock
to dive and fish from filled with bluegill, catfish, and frogs
turtles, ducks, snakes, muskrat, and heron
I was part of the wildlife just in my backyard
here, nature's drama was constantly unfolding
and I ran as untamed as the land

possessed
of an elfin wood-lore spirit
hopping rocks down gurgling ravines
catching crayfish and salamander barehanded
climbing trees and shaving my spears

making my sling from leather bootlaces
lord of my enchanted world
with my tawny German Shepherd,
Major
resembled the renowned Rin-Tin-Tin
playing with the little boy half his size
lolling his slobbery tongue
smiled, licking my dirty face til I threw
sticks he chased and chewed to straw
til his gums bled

next to me, Maj ran, grinning
in our wild outdoor freedom,
the guardian like a mother bear with the cub
killed snakes, whipping them side to side
in his wolfish teeth
before I met copper head
or water moccasin

we were easy
whether I pretended
to be an Indian or cowboy or spaceman
I could be anything and shapeshifted
leaping along in the forest

for I was a scrubby little woodland creature

_____

I'm a father of four with seven grandchildren. I lived overseas in
Africa and India for over twenty years. I was involved in
development work. I love to write and have a graphic
imagination. Allpoetry.com/Brian_Peter_Hodgkinson

[Stephen Hollins]

the silent cabin

the shadow of a wedge-tailed eagle
carries me into the jaws of a dark tunnel
brushing smooth the ribs of Sydney's Blue Mountain

steel clanks on the 1960 freight train
passing over thousands of pearl rosary beads
through airless silk black origami turns

steam wheels break at the cabin that grandfather built
split weatherboards freckled in rot
front red door dangles off rusted hinges

dust sieves through the remains of a brick chimney
where once autumn smoke billowed
from the log cabin, I was born in

on the homestead porch
Smiling-dog chews a turkey bone
inside the cabin music of heartbeats drum

our father ladles steaming pumpkin soup
grandad places plates on the tawa table
with a salad coloured in red and orange nasturtiums

grandma spreads yellow butter on brown rye bread
mother washes me in a red plastic tub
wrinkled feet splash bubbles, I gurgle

my two sisters play dress-ups on the stairs
the amber sun yawns goodnight
licking steamed-up windows

grandad lights a joke
father howls with laughter
grandma sings to me, as I jabber, jabber, jabber

silvery steel silence echoes up the spiral staircase
of my clay brain as I paint pictures of the family
I no longer have

I live on beautiful Waiheke Island in New Zealand. I specialize in
Improv for theatre, dance, clown, and mime, teaching adults to
become more playful, building, and being a dad.
Allpoetry.com/Stephen_Hollins

[Mark Van Loan]

Pennesseewassee Through Seasons

enter the sunlit timbers of Ordway Grove,
giant boulders and hemlocks guard
whorled wood asters and cinnamon ferns

white pines race to the spring blue sky,
a woodpecker rattles a hollow nearby
searching for food in the drumlike trunk

the roots of these trees run forever,
burrowing together like knotted fingers
that break the surface of the earth

we cross the rock wall to summer,
to birch trunks protruding from shallows,
moss creeping up their stick-like bones

we stand in a slight clearing of myriad trees,
the season sinking in with ticks and fleas,
white throated sparrows and chokeberries

I'd like to insert myself in a giant pine
stretch my branches in silver sunshine
feel the woodpeckers rattle my spine

we chew on a red leaf of wintergreen
happy with the minty flavor
smiling in summer's last moment

the sun recedes and we retreat from the lake,
into thickets that flame the fires of October,
into the burst and celebration of fall

embers reflect on the lake glass surface,
the invitation of the sundrenched deep
belies the shiver of the water

we wander from the leafless shores
towards thickets and needled paths,
breath plumes puffing in the crisp air

time moves us through seasons again,
into the frozen woods of tomorrow,
into the blustery months ahead

we watch the ice of these ancient waters
push slowly against the crusty banks,
limbs and trunks above swaying in silence

a thin dead tree spirals from the ground
like a ballerina with branches on top,
they curl like a dancer's graceful arms

running the strip at the back of Pike's Hill
you see the weary houses of the lake road,
punished by the wind and winters

Pennesseewassee is the "Big Lake"
freezing and thawing through time
patient and glistening beneath the jeweled foothills

I have had a career in technology and now I am moving towards a life of healing and writing. I have always written about nature and my love and concern for the environment and plan to publish in 2022. Allpoetry.com/Mark_Van_Loan

[Douglas Smith]

Wolfpack of Two

Howl at the moon
It's never too soon
In fact, it swoons
As the Alpha's growl consumes

Actually, counterintuitively
The dichotomy
Pushes, thrusts, pressed
Fighting, also going limp

Your musk
Is more attractive
Than lust
You must
Know this, me

———————————

I am trusting, ever loving, to the point of blindness. Might be a
crime thus, mindless love until you find one that reminds us you
deserve more. Much. A reminding crux, you're entitled to such.
Allpoetry.com/Djgs117

[Alwyn Barddylbach]

Morning River

Grose to Wiseman's Ferry
  amid the greening brown

Mirror
  mirror
in a
river,
  see me
  touch my
  waters clear,
on the
surface
watch me
  shimmer

ripples
never

  f
  r
  o
  w
  n

          Water
          water

in
a
mirror

wash me, clothe me like a rock,
catch my shadows in the skimmer

raindrops
never

d
r
o
w
n

Lighter
lighter
in the
shimmer,
raise me
float me
on a mirror,
cloud of
silky
reeds roll
under

boat
upon

a

morning

r
i
v
e
r

k a e r b e e r t m u g e h t d i m a

River
 river
 waters
deep,
 in wintry
  mirror's
 saddle
 cleave,
our god star
 dim in absence
 keep

reapers
never

 g
 r
 i
 e
 v
 e

Summer
falls from

hidden
hills

silver ghost on gibbous moon
morning rays cascade upriver

sun

on

spilt

l

a

g

o

o

n

s

Barking
cries
the burning
earth,
waning
quiet
waters frown,
auburn haze
in

morning
  dazzle

unwinding
  river

    d

    r

    o

    w

    n

Snowy-white
Eastern
  in the
    shade,
    oyster
    fields of
    pearly grey,
    sunlit mangroves
  on parade,
wading by
to Broken Bay

Upon the morning surf you
paint me blue, the ocean's maid

  river
river

nature
  mortal

  waters
  never

   f
a
d
  e

Every river has its course, where trails fade and its reach diminishes
- River reverie. The Hawkesbury, down river from Blue
Mountains, AB. Allpoetry.com/Barddylbach

[Ms. Norma-Jean Martin St. John]

Among Spring Meadowlarks

Among Spring coming periwinkle meadows
insulating miles of honeydew moss where a
pond known its reflecting woodside hills of the mountains of
prairies.

A flock of deer to their indigo floating waters
walking path trailing bordered with goldenrods and honey
suckers of the wild nature's sight covered rocks gunmetal landed.

Springtime brings shadowed over wavering
expansion beautiful blossoms of jade and plum trees with petals
fallen of the grounded earth in beautifully blown.

Night a watermelon sky revealing a buttery cinnamon clouds
where there is continuing found sight within a licorice darkened
stoned rays crossing the moon shown throughout crispy fallen air.

By morning yellowy stoned apple blooming shining blazing
butter sunflowers glowing and singing can be heard of blue jays in
the meadowlarks continues to hear beauty of woodpeckers
faraway drumming chilly hills.

The paths turning running rays of breezy air with bobbing of
children heads lightning shadows of the wildlife danced near
glowing honey smiling faces picnicking and playing of springtime
springing intoxicated outdoor fun.

Ms. Norma-Jean St John from Lynchburg Virginia; I have been a writer since I was young child. I been published since '2006' in several books and I have Gold Medals since '2013.' Writing is my passion. Allpoetry.com/Norma_St_John_Poetress

[Stephen Hollins]

the seagull

water laps and licks a salty tongue
inside oyster shells encrusted on the poles
that bear up the boathouse cafe
A floating seagull shrills like a meowing cat
its neck arches as it screams onto the surface of the sea

two grey-haired ladies yarn toffy English accents over
Putin's personality, the mystery of money, and rosariums
'Oh, I do so hate that ugly browning of my white JFK rose'
'Replace it dear, with Pope John Paul II, it's a vastly better bloom'

children wave from the bobbing pontoon, yelling
"Mum, it's going out to sea"
the grey-suited real estate woman "ahh-hars" into her iPhone
as her A4 pencil finger draws circles in the newspaper
the gull screams in animated metronome

kids run onto the cafe deck shouting
one of the ladies gasps "oh for heaven's sake!"
the masked waitress delivers a rocket, prawn, and halloumi salad
drizzled in balsamic and baby tomatoes

two toots pipe out from the car ferry
Its red metal hull slivers and twirls into the port
a tattooed Māori bone carver turns up her radio

as the commentator gathers momentum
whistles blow and the crowd cheers

sipping my second latte and Mrs. seagull is still
squawking in rhythm as the tea-green tide murmurs past
perhaps her webbed foot is tangled in a fishing line
does anyone else notice or even care?
meanwhile, a 3rd-generation home is blown to rubble
lines of police pepper spray the eyes of protestors
no one knows what to believe and politicians
play hide and seek

someone dressed exactly like me
bounces past the window
I realize I'm not a young man anymore
Pandora's glove punches me hard in the guts
legs stagger up to pay the bill, as I turn around
the devil in the Hokianga Harbour
(the final departing place of Kupe)
sleeks off in a Russian submarine
my friend the seagull
is nowhere to be seen
murders shadow lays upon my rest

———————————

I live on beautiful Waiheke Island in New Zealand. I specialize in
Improv for theatre, dance, clown, and mime, teaching adults to
become more playful, building, and being a dad.
Allpoetry.com/Stephen_Hollins

[Mark Van Loan]

Pachamama

have you seen the great layered locks
of Pachamama, floating around the globe
in plum and pink lavender braids

have you seen the jagged iced peaks
that reach for the sky from river blue basins,
crystals melting to clear surging streams

or the boiling and firing volcanoes
eliciting drops of rain from the swirling sky,
flames reaching like tongues for the heavens

see the bounty of patchwork fields bulging
with fruits, stretching like palm fronds
that jive and furl in hot equator winds

honor the gnarled boles of the green goddess,
bless the cool pulse of her dimpled stones,
hear the rhythm and surf of the sacred sea

now see the scorching of her forest lands,
feel the smothering of her boundless breath,
hear the furious cries of extinction
from the puncture of her fertile bulge

call on your mother oh amber eyed moon
tender the healing of mother's sweet womb

I have had a career in technology and now I am moving towards a life of healing and writing. I have always written about nature and my love and concern for the environment and plan to publish in 2022. Allpoetry.com/Mark_Van_Loan

[Marta Green]

Lonely Beaches

a hundred and fifty year old lighthouse
has outlived its usefulness
rusted body, creaky old grey stairs
once, painted a vivid white with blue stripes
now a smudge against the sea land scape
no more glowing light in the night from lanterns
even the keeper has vanished with time

ocean rise
the orphaned lighthouse is sinking
once in a while when the tide is out
visitors come to see this old relic
cameras, wondering who are in the photos on the walls
the smell of ancient metal and decay
still the scent of fish that had been cooked over the years

a little spooked at the silence
the group of on lookers
imagine they can see the old lighthouse keeper
opaque, dressed in period clothing, a black pipe in his mouth
whispering, of unknown origin, begins a mass tourist exodus

as the tide starts to come in and night falls on turbulent oceans
the new modern lighthouse, twenty miles away begins its watch
leading schooners, sail boats and yachts away from the rocky shore

splashed by ocean waves, sharp winds, whining structures forlorn, black against the sky, there seems to be one candle burning

---

Marta Green is from the state of Texas, about an hour from the gulf coast. She loves writing poetry and short stories. Her husband and family are some of her greatest supporters! Allpoetry.com/Marta_Green

[Stephen Hollins]

The Vertical Harp Plays Four Seasons

from the Medieval Orient,
commanding master Li He
'the demon talented one'
plays the same harp that the White Girl played
to the Yellow Emperor

each of the 24 strings is woven from the four seasons
its strands held tight in the arms of red hardwood
her ribbed arch stretches azure skies
clouds shuffle a slow tango
and fall away
to distant fields of amber wheat
chill winds whip the heartbeat

Le He hammers the strings
awakening the magician within
a tone shatters dense mountain jade
the snake goddess smelts stone
draws five colors to weld the broken sky
where the demon punched a hole
stones split wide, jarred heavens shake
autumn leaves let down rain
phoenixes screech, perfumed orchids bloom
lotuses stream chill teardrops
primeval fish skim above waters
and bony dragons dance

music melts the cold driblets of light
colors play hopscotch to unfold winters tail
fireflies illuminate the twelve city gates
the moon cupped in the sun's silver shadow
swings the axeman to catch
her tumbling music

I live on beautiful Waiheke Island in New Zealand. I specialize in
Improv for theatre, dance, clown, and mime, teaching adults to
become more playful, building, and being a dad.
Allpoetry.com/Stephen_Hollins

[Mark Van Loan]

last dawn on Cobscook Bay

I found a wishing stone on Jasper beach
a small red angled rock with three white stripes
a trinity of perfect seams
layers of sediment and history forged through time

the beach was filled with smooth round rhyolite stones
and white rocks with pepper-like pockmarks
the surf tumbled and ground the balls across the expanse

green moss out the windows and rain on the cottage roof
gusts and sheets tapping across the weathered shingles
in the last dawn on Cobscook Bay

Ross Cottage flickered with kerosene lamps while the big black
cast iron stove, the Kineo Star, crackled in the down poor
old books and navigation maps shadowing pine wood walls

you can feel the energy of the channels that course throughout the
bay
floating the rockweed up and down in the never-ending tide
eating away the red rock cliffs of East Bay and Rogers Point

an eagle circled above the cliffs and the hummingbird
swooped by to check for sugar water in the feeder
birds of prayer on the porch with spider web corners
and Canadian flag shaped railings

we found chunky green sea glass and barnacled beach rocks
some with long clumps of rockweed hanging from them like hair
from gnarled old heads, barnacles like cancer on the cheeks

sleek black cormorants raced across the water
long slender bodies gliding gracefully beneath curved
arching wings of power and beauty
framed against eastern reflections of early golden light

we walked down the giant slab rock stairs to the beach
and the fabled stone bridge by the spring, on the path
to the moss myth forest and the bay of scallop shells

all of this beauty and the breathless tides that rise in me
the channels that flow across the bays of justice in my spirit
aghast at the ecocide I see in this land of sacred beauty

weep for the rockweed of these boundless suffering waters
weep for the tons thieves whisk away
raping the tender habitat that shelters and feeds the living bay

dream again of free-flowing waters
of the breathing of the bay through night and day
osprey circling red cliff shores and kingfishers hovering
over high tide waters, arching for the last graceful dive

—————————————

I have had a career in technology and now I am moving towards a
life of healing and writing. I have always written about nature and
my love and concern for the environment and plan to publish in
2022. Allpoetry.com/Mark_Van_Loan

[Kristy Holtum]

Blood moon rises a rarity

the full moon is softer in line with the sun
bloodshed tinge of dusk
kisses her glowing crown
highlighting her pearling features

fruitful agents sitting across the bay
waiting for movement
waiting for the weather to travel back
into arm's reach

big shy eyes
rose-tinted brightness and lava-full lips
the pulsing meeting ground of starlight

nights occurrence is
posing planets
shine mandarin ripeness
streaming Jupiter like waves of auburn sky
that fall behind her orange-toned evening

motions capture the month
starlight fading into bright sparks
following the shadows
of the fallen sun
down the edge of hillsides

passing moonbeams
etching me in a grieved sky

stretching black into secondary sparks
shallow whispers fade into willows
leaning westward

parting flags of yesterday fade into detail
pale cheeks now a shade of red
and winter frost setting in my hand
bites of sea breeze sing me to breathe death
the night air hunts a broken beat in the dark

black feathered canvas
splattering dusk lower
staining hands and toes
horizontal viewing
night songs fly to the clock tower
chiming twelve screeching wings
rising into a written dawn
scattering vowels
thousands of seconds to light
death shall hold memories in stone

reflecting on the sunset back
gazing at autumn's grieved view
as it tints the stone in crimson waves
they touch the tips of dusks memory
then fade

maple shadows line the shore
the soiree of dusk bending and turning
she leans into the night
with bright orange hair
prowling like a lioness of the horizon
hunting daydreams in the early hours
she weaves through the patchwork of day
kissing the light left-back in younger eyes
cutting pages blend with the darker side
the artists smudge heartbeats

reading the week's itinerary
of moon journeys
aiming for starlight
waiting for midnight like sub-ins
on the bluestone pavement
players in groups
of blinking lights
travelling the smokey tips of age

she is autumn unfolding into firelights
now it is dark
viewing winter passengers in the side space
a kiss of goodnight from her orange tinge

strolling sun blast views
to the wrinkled sandy isles
blushing pale face turning to the tide
blowing kisses off the mountain top

a grieved glance as the sky shows her dark side
turning cherry plum red

———————————

Krissi is an Australian poet born July 5th 1978 in Dandenong, Victoria. Moved to Townsville Queensland in her mid-30s. Krissi's poetry is influenced by nature, music and her surroundings. Allpoetry.com/Krissi_Holtum

[Sally Clark]

Enigmatic Ellipsis

Cinderella-starved
ruby cobwebs
splintered synapses shriek
gauzy misfirings
fuel someone else
dart gasp gulp dig clasp.

Crucifixion cracks bone marrow grins
as bloodless knuckles
clench in synch
with pitted teeth,
exposing snow-capped
cavernous amber coffer,
this sacred land mine.

Massacred mentality
single-handed
sun-scorched someday
horizon materializing
dimmed rays, dampened doom
fairy godmother
pharmaceutical screenplay.

Threadbare throat
tick-swallow-tock
stroke of somnolent surge

exhale at last as slippered glass
grants breath,
three hours at best.

Plastic smack of lips
suckle-sputter
handmade quicksand

———————————

Smc resides in USA.

Pain is the pen that purges my past and carves a path towards the
promise of a tomorrow. Allpoetry.com/smc

[JC Anger]

shattered glass

chalk skirts the sidewalk in the pastels
Pepto Bismol pink and the Easter egg blues
my child's hand, the vapor holding the blunt pieces
scratches on the chipped surface

all that remains are the marble stones
and the cemetery plots
my father, brother, mother and daughter
below in the potting soil

what flowers grow
from the walls of the steel caskets?

pinewood floorboards
the seat for the blind soldier
end table, the bourbon drink stand
cracked picture frames
scrolled in the finger flits

vapors ascending in the smokestack exhales
passing the salmon cracked lips
into the mold tinted air

search my brain for the castaway thoughts

friend's face
tattooed in the eyelids

his blood stained the Arabian Desert
130 plus degrees Fahrenheit
Taps played as the rifles charged
sleeping a half mile from grandfather

piqued sips from the tourist shot glass
a gulp, the throw, the shatter
scream at the smoke stained eggshell wall
the loudest silence breaking the night

life whispers the deaf requiems
to the ears of the blind soldier

death makes me whole

A 3rd generation war veteran who uses poetry as support for
neurologic and mental conditions associated with the war and life.
JC is a self-taught poet, loves fishing and treasure hunting
Allpoetry.com/JCA

[Bill La Civita]

Stone Pillars

I settle flanked by hoodoos
cut by wind and rain
and watch the misty waterhole's oily sheen

I play with the fallen verdure strewn across the ground
invoking myriad specters the emperors of the pond

spirit of the lake come forth
flaunt your woven aqua-robe
flicker through a wrinkle in the fabric of space-time

my rhythmic singing totters and instead
unleashes the watchmen of the pillars

these misanthropic troglodytes entomb me in their home
with no air to sip or sun to glimpse
huffing clammy slime and mud
atomic beasts enchain me

inside this damp cemented web
the decades slip
one afternoon and evening fade
before I stumble back to town

those summoned gnomes unseen
now shadow me

but their geometry entangles souls
no sacrament expels them

I conjure my queer qualities
stone configurations in the wood
that crystallize my countenance
stone-faced and unrepentant

———————————

Retired, gay, married, working-class: I have been writing poetry
for years, but I have not displayed it until now. My influences are
William Carlos Williams, Kenneth Rexroth, Emily Dickerson, etc.
Allpoetry.com/Blll

[Joel Mazo]

Returning

As I walked the path to Lola Fe's house
to return grass scissors borrowed
to give order to my hedge,
I noted the scissors well used on her own.
The couch grass crawled leisurely and orderly.
The protruding antenna grasses lopped off.
The bushes formed fine quadrilaterals
that spoke of the industry of the old matron.
The cut twigs were gathered in a neat heap.
There were no broken shells of hermit crabs
that littered the sea road I crossed:
victims of vicious playfulness of sea children.
The stone wall like an arm
that kept things from growing out of reach,
like these grass scissors that now returned,
like heavenly wanderers rolling in orbits
but keep their places near the sun.
We must return all things.

––––––––––––––

A graduate of Bachelor of Theology from Adventist University of the Philippines. Has been writing poetry from his youth. He lives in Pampanga, Philippines with his wife and four children.
Allpoetry.com/Joel_Mazo

[Douglas Smith]

Exciting Unknown

How did we
Why did we
Where did we
Come to this junction?

Allowing me
Entrapping me
Inviting me
Become one with you?

Surrounding us
Bounding us
Inclining us
To go from one to two?

That answer is lost in cosmos.
Beautifully, most.

———————————

I am trusting, ever loving, to the point of blindness. Might be a crime thus, mindless love until you find one that reminds us you deserve more. Much. A reminding crux, you're entitled to such. Allpoetry.com/Djgs117

[Robert Murray Smith]

Sacred Earth

as night drew its last gasp
sounds of a new day played
kookaburras and magpies' call

an explosion in the fresh air
red, orange and white clouds
billowing like the first dawn

the high country revived day
in its steamed air so fresh
whitened by its muddy snow

awaiting yellow sun flares
magpie brumbies' steamed flanks
started to stir, loud neighs, shaking

the cold air startled by anticipation
taking off as one, hooves flying
uprooting sacred earth, trampling

exquisite plants thrown into the air
the brumbies just living like horses
downward they flowed excitedly

a helicopter whirred, shots rang out
one after the other they fell
to overpopulation, and being unwelcome

My poetry is eclectic. However, I have a great interest in the mind, and the Big Bang. I try in each poem to better the last.
Allpoetry.com/Robert_Murray_Smith

[Robert Ray]

anonymous was a woman

after the Natascha Graham painting

your mother once called you a spring flower.
the talk: the birds and the bees—and the snakes.

over the threshold you looked for rainbows.
that stone-wall trellis is an explosion
of wisteria. (the demons still sneak in.
for *a long life* and *immortality* ,

the florist lied.) you preferred red tulips.
in april rain, i see purples and blues.
i'm not crazy; you're not in the frame.
you never stood naked in the garden.

(the woman's hip is missing your birthmark.)

truth: there is no garden, no wisteria,
no flowers beyond those french doors.
an obelisk stands, other side of town;
red poppies wreathe oak trunks the rains turn black.

on the sill, the silk tulips stay red and inodorous.
a multichromatic hematoma
spreads like kudzu on stone, the king coils in fronds, gulls
squawk. confused, one bee sees a budding rose.

i swat erratically and shoo it—
away from the rendering, into the sunlight.

––––––––––

Robert E. Ray's poetry has been published by Rattle, Beyond
Words International Literary Magazine, Wild Roof Journal, and
The Ekphrastic Review. He lives in coastal Georgia.
Allpoetry.com/R.E._Ray

[Stephen Hollins]

beach battlefield

wealthy wage war   t   poor die

shining steel   teeth bite

metal oil fire   explodes

radio calls   voice unseen

par a chute hang s   empty cage

kepis march   sandy fields

crimson   footprint disappears

barbed-wire   blow flies sing

whistling crack   ear drums bleed

flapping white   blue and red

rosalie bayonet   helmet stands

cracked l i p s   cigarette smokes

all men are brothers   (so they say)

stake honor_____ freedom song

frontline tactician   military maze

napoleon bon a par te   joan of ark

dogs fight   like the lion

for a colored   piece of ribbon

leo tol stoy   marks this page

seize mo ments   of hap piness

love   loved

and be

all else is fucking folly!

all_____   folly!

I live on beautiful Waiheke Island in New Zealand. I specialize in Improv for theatre, dance, clown, and mime, teaching adults to become more playful, building, and being a dad.
Allpoetry.com/Stephen_Hollins

[Charles B. Carr]

looking glasses

As it happens,
every day is earth day,
it's just late April
has the edge of spring
in its step. Forsythias
pack up their fanfare,
hardwoods fill in
the gaps where heat
escaped winter; maple
leaves are the smallest
hands it takes to reach
little things:
dogwoods bloom like new
batches of stars
get their wings, grasses
scatter the colors of chasing
rabbits, an early frog
clears its throat, several insects
stretch their legs, birds, bees,
a Mother can't decide
if whistle or hum is best
to muffle the drums
from a species
whose interests are not
at the heart of a planet

48

and if thought is
what counts, the sun
on branches of autumn olive
is as good as goldfinches
are a place to start.

My wife and I have finally realized our dream of a mountain by
the river; the poetry there writes itself, I do what I can to put it to
words. Allpoetry.com/selfrisinmojo

[Susan A Szoke]
harvest moon passages

fall chills tremble throughout rural veins
as earth offers her dulcet morning song
cathedral glass splashes over her mantle
the rich colors appliquéd to dawn's hillsides

red-shouldered hawks circle high above
a mated pair of raptors searching for food
doves and thrushes engage in polite chatter
mulberry shadings pulse with busy blackbirds
sorting out their breakfast choices al fresco

a lone farmer drives his truck on rutted roads
his best friend seated to his right with fur flying
companionable silence fills the bouncing cab
as the labrador shifts to drink in stiff breezes

tonight a harvest moon casts silver shadows
farmhouse lights paint ghostly whited branches
while two buddies drift off to dreamland
one canine head resting on a human foot

———————————

New to poetry three years ago, I am driven to write as a widely
varied outlet for self-expression and healing. Native to Florida,
US, I am an avid gardener, nature lover and lover of people.
Allpoetry.com/GardenDelights

[Robert Poleski]

Night of passion

e.e. cummings flavor

serendipitous meet
an evening stroll (it was raining a little).

girl's tall with the longing eyes
hard body filled with surprise
(behind the hard long smile
she stands on her long hard legs.
asks me to go with her...
the rain starts pouring).

Invites, come into her house,
touch...
her
mind--
write a poem
(but her long legs... begin
heaveandtwine about
me, lips kiss my face) ---

--- the night's
thick-like-fog(no more rain).
in the darkness. irises meet.
(blue-laser-beams dim the starlight,blush on the moon's face)

Savor-the-breath(the honey mingled with water)
the twin peaks gleaming
ridges.(Vesuvius and Etna)
the Eros' winds (whip the crest, strike the matchstick.ignite
supernova)
naked kisses.
maelstrom.

kiss up and down the slopes
heaps and thighs (explore, the poem. the undiscovered country
untouched by the sun)
fingernails run the seam
(carve blood seals on the belly).
Tongue sucks gold(probes deep-sea fishes in Marianas Trench;
the salt on the lips)

   --- inflames
the straw trigger.
sets off fire, the flames,dance
around the wick;
fingers crowd on the violin neck.
fiddlehead(the slick seed of pomegranate);
tune it up(the tongue recites the revelation book).

the volcano err...
rrupts!, the goose...
bumps...
ex!
plode!...

--mind. the earthquake epicenter--
                touched
d
r
o
w
n

---The Poem Is Written
The burning bush --
embers dim.

coiled---
    (tucked in each other's sweat)
cooling off--
        lay
breath...
...less---

  ---- waiting... to... resurface.

(readying for the follow-up)

_____

What I see is my own world, my whole intimate universe, with
my mind, my heart, looking inside things, inside feelings, what
makes it laugh or cry, love or hate, what makes it feel pleasure or
pain. Allpoetry.com/Robert_Poleski

[Robert Poleski]

Enter the storm

it's coming

breakers crash
cavernous bowels stir
the hissing sea lashes pebbles back and forth
a raspy rumbling echo rolls through the air
a tremulousness to fear
waves slobbering with salty lips
pound into the cliff
rip-tide rolls heave and extinguish its rage

it's here

"the turbid ebb and flow of human misery"
suppurating hatred of the sea
sounds of dark thoughts cold as ghoul's eyes
a spectre's cloak
hides heaven and earth from the view
echoing waves
free from the bondage of words
hold memories of martyrs

aftermath

marooned on the forsaken cay
subsistential marshland
riparian-dark holm
find the trail of Exodus
through the red sea of faith
sea of the Ark
the swallowing Jonah belly
full of tempests unexpected squalls
life's beginnings and endings

What I see is my own world, my whole intimate universe, with
my mind, my heart, looking inside things, inside feelings, what
makes it laugh or cry, love or hate, what makes it feel pleasure or
pain. Allpoetry.com/Robert_Poleski

[Ms. Norma-Jean Martin St. John]

Seasonal Beautiful of Trees

Tree land woodside, roadsides, parks views
lined the mountain tops
the absentee in thy trees
words of sight the planting to bring new life

harvest fruits orchard into the farmlands
southern countrywide hillsides gritty and dirty
swinging the Tarzan rope to rope across ponds ~
climbing trees to the top meet the race

as the boys makes a tree fort spying on the girls
while the girls make a play house hanging curtains;
in the night they scare the boys in bear sounds
while birds singing the gears the nestling their nest

feeding new baby birds as their mouth openings
words the works living in the trees
catching leaves and poking stones bathing ponds
hide-and-seek running in the woods 'till sundown

moonlit the skies between the veins
plant maker hear a prayer to save our
burch, aspen, pine, apple, bonsai,
redwood, sapling, forest, lone elm ~

orchard trees from being destroyed in
destruction of hot flames fires burning logs
save our trees today; tomorrow viewing from log cabins builts
watches them continue enjoy the shade beauty ~

changing seasonal hours the yearly freedom ...

Ms. Norma-Jean St John from Lynchburg Virginia; I have been a
writer since I was young child. I been published since '2006' in
several books and I have a Gold Metal since '2013.' Writing is my
passion Allpoetry.com/Norma_St_John_Poetress

[Ms. Norma-Jean Martin St. John]

Love Thy Love

love thy love ~
one kingdom spreads petals wings
the drapes babybreathe darkness
your face flown of wildflowers

forest wilderness deepest mane
birds filled the slept skeletons
while thy breast are swan black
and yellow leather

upon thy whispering treasures
driveway the boost of thy kissed lipstick lips
bough of me bough of November falls
approach of falling those armpits arms

thighs to holden white wagon train to the
prince charming of queens
stripes of red minsel toes mindsets
always wanted voice to sang to you

love thy love
into thy mouth to thy head is a bells of chimes
pleasant valley of golden ring to wear
my hear of hairstyles is as soldier

warrior's sword
defense of defeated defaults
an army of many shoulders
trumpets sounded of victorious victory

shall thy whispered trees arms of winds into
a dreaming armies arms
whom seed as if fruit is painless
thought of not

thy lips saddles of fire glossy scarlett
upon who kiss upon thy combine of
kings and queens intoxicated love
written fingers of twists

are holy hands of God's goodness
therefore kept to the depths keying
in thy bloodthirsty
thy footsteps into the anklets are

washed of ashes in ~
rivers banks stillwater's mountain streams
onto flower bedspreads of painted golden
I'm thy glowing stars of shimmer blown trims

lit the mist dances darkness skylight starlight fired
drumming beating belt into thy eyed momently
dreams of bells rings wonderlands increased
aroma equally desirable one's eventide mist

Ms. Norma-Jean St John from Lynchburg Virginia; I have been a writer since I was young child. I been published since '2006' in several books and I have a Gold Metaler since '2013.' Writing is my passion Allpoetry.com/Norma_St_John_Poetress

untitled #13

looking backward
from the outside in
fields of coriander
stand between us

rows of green beans
and stalks of corn
patterning
the passing pictures

moving past
the window seat viewfinder
whipping past
your breezy hair
flapping in the aerodyne

hand-painted yellow
Lego building blocks
divide us
from incoming
snake oil tanker trucks

but the dried squares
are never enough
to keep us safe

and prevent us
from fixating backwards

miles are to be harvested
long before moonshine
now hanging on stakes to dry
before the crimson sunrise
in the West Virginian
za za clouds

falling from the sky
in plain view

_____

A plain-clothes engineer, writer, artist, and general over-thinker
wrapped into one epithelial sheet deemed human.

I have coined the theme of my work as 'Bio-organic surrealism'.
Allpoetry.com/Colvet

[George L. Ellison]

The life and death of a Mountain Spring

Water is but a gentle trickle
emerging from rocks
as a mountain spring
clean and pure
it begins to fall
down mountainsides
sleek and tall

Down it falls
through hill and dale
cutting a swathe
the length of its trail
full of life in many forms
see the angler wait
with his tin of worms

On she goes
through leafy wood
where native flowers
come into bud.
Over falls,
weirs and eddies
still so pure
though turning muddy

Past fallen trees
wrecks of cars
boxes tins
empty jam jars
the flotsam of life
is nowhere better mirrored
than a walk beside streams
as they turned into rivers

The river meanders
through village town and city
becoming more polluted
it is such a pity
that man cannot clean up his act
but just blunder blindly on
till the river
isn't so much water
but more pollution

The river becomes an estuary
flowing further out to sea
the sea dilutes the toxic waste
though it's still there
for sea-life to taste

It eventually breaks up
sufficiently
as it gets further out to sea

Let us hope there is no oil spill.
Pollution is such a bitter pill

I have written poetry all my life but mainly since 1994 when I
really started to take it seriously
I have always enjoyed english language and literature
and generally enjoying life as I live it

Allpoetry.com/Queserasera

[Christine Weber]
Natalie's Ashes

we scattered Natalie's ashes
from a motor boat
stilled in the ocean
soft breeze
like a flick of a hand
Anacapa Island Arch
seen in the distance
tilted half oval space
with a cut off torso above
two strong rock leg sides
capped by icing
made of bird droppings
radiant sun kissing it's reflection
on the mirrored water
long and rippled
sky bright blue
as a newborn child's eyes
ocean suspending
waves like blanket wrinkles
denting the water
holding a body
contained in a tube
made to quickly dissolve
dropped slowly by son
last touch

fingers letting go
followed by
fragrant red roses and yellow daisies
clung together like family
gulls screeching above
wet faces
memories
photographs
fragrances of scenes past
disappearing from surface
sparkling ashes glistening underwater
goodbye, sunlight lady

I am a traveling grandmother, poet, artist, and Ukulele player. I
didn't know I could write poetry that people would enjoy reading
until I joined Allpoetry! Allpoetry.com/ChrisW

[David I Mayerhoff]

The Stormy Sea

The boat rocks and sways
in the dark of night
wind howling like in Chiller Theatre
no sight of the living for miles
by the light of the crescent moon

creaking and banging
sailor Tom spits up his lunch
working on dinner

foam in the water
the sea covered with vomit
heaving towards the weary crew

sailor Pete down below
hears the hull bang
as the boat smacks each wave
and all tremble

to be lost at sea
not to be heard from again

if only we knew
when our last gasp will be
we could prepare properly

and set the table of life
with our finest
a proper sendoff
for a life well lived

no regret or neurotic caution
living on our terms
exiting by the ocean's

the 28 foot cabin cruiser
swallowed whole
I hope the sea doesn't choke

—————————————

David I Mayerhoff is an emerging literary writer, established
scientific author, and a Clinical Professor of Psychiatry. He grew
up on Long Island and now resides in New Jersey.
Allpoetry.com/David_Mayerhoff

[David I Mayerhoff]

Bull Rush

I will overwhelm you with my stadium dazzle
not take no for an answer
let subtlety take a back seat
far away at the corner dump

the sheer raw power of the linebacker
mowing down all in his path
the lineman, bugs, overgrown grass
opening the angle to the quarterback

LA Rams meet the Cincinnati Bengals
welcome to the party
in the elevated castle of the mundane

contradictions are straightaways
smooth is jagged
and the linoleum floor
is a rough tarp

if you are hungry for dainties
the pastries are next door
here it is raw meat
set oven to zero

don't like the menu?
I am not fond of your attire
deal with it

if you are looking for the school choir
you sir, are in the wrong zip code
area code
whatever

we are not here to mince words
but to mincemeat
chop up the enemy
let him chew cabbage
why?
because i am not fond of cabbage

chew on that

———————————

David I Mayerhoff is an emerging literary writer, established scientific author, and a Clinical Professor of Psychiatry. He grew up on Long Island and now resides in New Jersey.
Allpoetry.com/David_Mayerhoff

[James Hartley]

Manolete's Dying Words: A Year In

Madrid

Summer bisects sidewalks:
in the shade old José shuffles breadwards.
Between bollards, street bleached bright.
Against red wood plaza walls, the bull slumps, bleeds, dies.
Lovers writhe on swimming pool lawns:
skies shine, shutters clatter down.

Winter brings the Burberry out.
El Retiro's boat tank clinks with ice.
Snow slices free sierra passes.
Old José rocks with Ana, his wife,
before a floating fire of forms - screams, eyes -
waiting for grandkids, TV on.
Fingers touching. Quiet. Calm.

Spring dries up the reams of rain,
draws out the shades, ups José's grin.
Ana's chair unfurls in the sunny street,
beach beer-baptised, heat throbbed beats;
skin once occluded bathed in light
tables on pavements - cañas, wine -
black glinting glass, cloudless sky.

Jose falls, another leaf,
Ana's arms a bare elm tree.
Below a wind-streaked, breaking sky -
Madrilenean square, autumn morning.
The seasons in José's open eyes.
Genuflecting, Ana sighs,
kisses his bald, grey head, distraught -
'All for nought, cariño', she whispers,
'All for nought, all for nought.'

James Alexander Hartley (Liverpool, England, UK, 10 May 1973)
lives and works in Madrid, Spain with his wife Ana and two
children Carmen Elise and Matty. Allpoetry.com/J._A._Hartley

[Elise Gordon]

Tracks

As steel wheels pound down the rails
I feel dwarfed standing alongside
baritone vibrations jangle at my innards
until I oscillate at the same frequencies

Shiny black titans emit steam and whistle
as steel coupling joins heavy segments
these behemoths link east=west=north=south
and the landscape is crisscrossed into puzzle pieces

With the stench of fuel, oil and lube
these hardened beasts take on our burdens
what a work of our imagination and hands
a fine metallic symphony roars on the tracks...

_____

My writings are snippets of observations, meditation, release,
wordplay. The Pacific Northwest is beautiful, inspiring and so
glad to call it home. Allpoetry.com/SunsOnFire

[Mark Van Loan]

silver drop

robins chirp shrilly in the cold pre-dawn
earth of April reticent and frosted
life crouches and waits in the deep

trees take shape in the umbral light
the moon wanes and winks in the maya blue sky
time is but a whisper of our pulse

the sun rises in tangerine smiles
fire rages in the kiln of the dream
my trail is blazed by the burn of belief

daybreak dew glistens and drips
pools gather from the growing steam
existence bulges in the silver drop

I have had a career in technology and now I am moving towards a life of healing and writing. I have always written about nature and my love and concern for the environment and plan to publish in 2022. Allpoetry.com/Mark_Van_Loan

[Syed Buali Gillani]

A swamp of words

Translations:
Lost in that moment of decade long bliss,
statically frozen in time
waiting for your fingertips to move
From my neck to your hair.

Dialectical materialists:
Cheap wine and passing days
Passing. Mountains of ash,
walking forests and flying fishes
roses growing upon thorns
in London "the rich man's empty pocket".
Drunk rotten voices fill the air
dark narrow streets, new and neat
tall empty churches.
And something says that far away,
over the hills and far away
In rich heavy soil, infested with small brisky rats
a farmer wishes to dig his children's grave.
His eyes can see past
beyond and deep within the souls of hypocrites
but he remains hidden
under the mist. Under the smoke
of a thousand cigarettes,
which he wears like a night gown
as he knows,
He knows that to live means to see.

Forgotten selves:
And I see this man standing,
as he whispers to himself with a ripe tongue
sharp as a sword, hot like a flame
"The moon is black with judgment"
The hour of Judgment has come
for my flesh and stretched bones,
my eyes mute with fierce wrath
and God whispers to me:
"You are he who is not, I AM HE WHO IS."
Judgment has come for me,
Death has come for me.
There is no where else to hide
no star that I do not fear
with terror and contempt.

We reached the heavens
where I hoped the waters would be blue
like the Mediterranean.
They are black like night-waters and moon
Blood: but between, I saw a ferry-man stand,
spitting words into the sea:
"O you old soulless body; dead among the living".

———————————

Syed is an Urdu and Farsi language poet who recently published
his first English poetry book called "A Poet's Heart". Aside from
poetry he is interested in philosophy & psychology.
Allpoetry.com/Syed_Buali_Gillani

[S. Libellule]

Click Baiting

What is it with this place...
billionaire men pissing all over space
meanwhile down below women lug water
for hours to boil... (not even for two thirds pay)

While those who are "free"
seek out their addictions
their dopamine benedictions
Halo, fb, Cuba Libre, Oxy, ESPN

Just more bread and circus
for each of us
while we await the fiddler
to strike the megaton match

Tallying all these clicks
counting all these licks
to the center of a Tootsie Pop
multitasking blizzard of a daze

As the Russian stack dolls
topple on over
crushing Ukrainian clover

just to see the "Like" button

Originally from New England, Libellule currently lives outside of Birmingham, Alabama. Poetic influences include Mary Oliver, Billy Collins and ee cummings.   Allpoetry.com/Little_Dragonfly

[Lonna Lewis Blodgett]

First Dance

The sHy FiRSt dANce

Red sa@@shes
S + Way from your cheeeks
b.l.u.r.r.i.n.g your
f+Hair skin
shineee In the DARKNEST
FLAshhhH of
s*e*q*u*i*n*e*d   Light
ur eyes
I cant seem to find
UUUUUU
Shimmmmmmmying in the BRunette
C Peeking
oVer=== SUBSTITUTE windows
T h e s e con jurors """sing"""
UTT er vo-ice
of DIS&&&&TRACTION
B cuz .... I whirlllll!
In;;;;;;;;;;to
O-u-t of con-trol
trOUBLE
Ant Sy JiTt ers
Milk^^^shake m e l t s
in>>>>to your ChASsis
po..........king

my stom ache j # uices
I CANT FIND^^^^^ my leggggggs
How can
EYEcandy d+ance

With((((((Red Sashes

———————————

I have spent a lifetime searching for truth and meaning. I have
found in the art of poetry the uniqueness of intrinsic language as
the conveyance of the human experience.
Allpoetry.com/Lonna_Lewis_Blodgett

[Vicki Moore]

Orange

I watch the glistening glow of a late day sun
as it streaks across the sky in hues of orange;
red mixing with yellow, blending together.
Odd shaped bubbles of juice, covered by skin,
burst open, exploding orange into my mouth,
and sometimes stinging as it spurts into my eyes.
I let the peels fall to the summer dry ground,
curling bits of life for my tabby to play with.
In the autumn, the leaves of my oak tree
will turn orange, falling to carpet the ground.
Flames flicker in the cold Halloween night,
tucked inside the Jack-O-Lantern I carved,
leading the children to the sweet treats on my porch.
On the coldest night in winter I still sit outside,
the air freezing my breath as I exhale,
bundled up in my old orange and yellow blanket,
leftover from the time I decorated my bedroom
with golden sunflowers and bright tiger lilies.
The blue sparks dance towards the night sky,
leaping from the orange glow of the fire I sit beside.
In my yard, spring brings Orioles and robins
to gather by the bird feeders I fill every day.
Grosbeaks and Tanagers fill the air with song.
Marigolds, Tulips, and Gerbera daisies break ground,
inviting the bees to feast inside their beauty.

I can live without many things,
but not without the color orange.

———————————

I am a 61 year old woman who has been through a lot in my life.
Poetry helps me to process, heal, and even appreciate my past.
Allpoetry.com/Vicki_moore

[Andrew Huang]

Carousel

batting lights on scrolled cresting begin
to bokehly blur, as porcelain horses gallop
floridly to band organs and cymbals.
we remain dreamily in each other's hold,
witnessing the feverish horses floating—
gilded night too spins brilliantly in circle.

we pass the ticket booth where long line
seems shorter now than at the beginning.
bells and whistles cheer at passing floats.
pastel horses in garland robes gallop
in place, trying to escape from the hold.

we nest in our carriage, as we briefly lose
ourselves to the horses pacing along a line,
becoming unaware these frenzy gallops
are leading us back to an idle beginning—

where blowing pipes sign a gradual end.
we can only hope that we do not lose
the lulling sights of these horses galloping.

our carriage curbs tamely; the horses trot.
we open our eyes as we slow to an end—

we open our eyes as we slow to an end.

Andrew Huang, also known as Change, is a poet from San Francisco, CA. He discovered poetry in high school, and since then honed his skills through various workshops and English writing classes. Allpoetry.com/Ah.Changeoo

[Vivian Nguyen]

Autumn's Houses

There are two houses on top of grass,
which then have a lake seem as glass.
Graceful is how liquid in nice shape,
elegant whence classic landscape.

That white house looks like a mansion,
since it looks so huge, with expansion.
So then that red house is very small,
indeed it is tiny, being on season fall.

Brown leaves are beside a giant tree,
a mailbox is open with as mail to see.
Autumn does have that timber imply,
ergo that wood seems just as high.

As for fall is being expressed then,
due to that weather looks to when.

———————

All of my poems would just have 100 words each. I do have most
of my poems to be rhyming, but then some are in free verse. That
could be for me to like rhyming poetry inside my contests.
Allpoetry.com/ThisVyoletter

[Marta Green]

The Orange Orchard

fragrant orange perfume (wafting through the air)
a sunny day in the southern California - Orange Orchards
10 lbs of fruit -- for 3 dollars

walking throooogh the Orchard
a smatttering of oranges on rich fertile soil;
perfect circular O

I pluck a succulent fruit
peeling in a spiral Z like a stair case unraveling
biting into orange tinged translucent liquid
drips down my chin like a cool, refreshing """"""" rain storm

driving away, sloooowly, the Orchard fades in my rear view
mirror

––––––––––––––

Marta Green is from the great state of Texas where she lives with
her husband. She has three sons and 2 daughters. Her passion has
always been writing, reading and art.
Allpoetry.com/Marta_Green

[Leah Johnson Lee]

The Undermost

Disconnected from
the outlet
can you
measure the
distance back
to the
plug in
the static
of droning
sound. You
have paddled
into the
bald chatter
a treeless
forest for
prayers sake
combing over
empty follicles
turning up
nothing but
electric dust.
This place,
the undermost
of a
drain, the

thin metal
tone, the
oxycalcium ozone
you cannot
crawl from.

[David I Mayerhoff]

In Sync Dance and Tune

the bushes flow with the breeze
stutter step right cha cha left
the great tree swoons with the rhythm of the backyard garden
a central figure in the orchestra
bark to bark
the many branches rustling wind instruments

the wind howls harmony-
a flutist is that i hear?

the grass sways back and forth
speed to its advantage
plants at the boundary divide
moving to the groove
neither slow nor bulky

the disco replete with the seductive
the elegant
the clod and the nimble of foot

as i enter the backyard
I can't help but join the boogie
shuffling to the right
in sync to the left
my own Studio 54

dancers all decked out
in their finest party threads

looking up at the great conductor
in the vast expanse of blue sky
hoping that the doors to this disco are kept open
and the price of admission doesn't change

––––––––––––––––––

David I Mayerhoff is a literary writer, established scientific
author, and a Clinical Professor of Psychiatry. He grew up on
Long Island and now resides in New Jersey.
Allpoetry.com/David_Mayerhoff

[Robert Poleski]

Melancholy in blue

On the painting: Morning at the beach - Trish Vevera

missing you-
as the dawn raises
water turns to air
as life turns to breath
in a fierce embrace
urging matter upwards
where the energies of earth begin-
zinc and lead and chrome
turn into the blue sea and sky-
await the sun
to purge the heart's darkness

the limitless horizon's arch disappears in space
burned spirit
    paints skies changing hues
waves are sleepy in their liquid robes-
seagulls arrow swiftly through the air-
lonely frigate rests by the lighthouse
anglers on the shore
    catch the zephyr breeze
refreshing mist of salty droplets
    on their faces-
the homeward air
spray-paints Van Gogh's symphony

of a lonely heart
on a cerulean blue brim

What I see is my own world, my whole intimate universe, with
my mind, my heart, looking inside things, inside feelings, what
makes it laugh or cry, love or hate, what makes it feel pleasure or
pain. Allpoetry.com/Robert_Poleski

[Anna Gopen]

tangerine

'tangerine,' you whispered while
strumming hands across my hair
as though these strands
made music   as sweet as their namesake

the sunset blazes
through your fingers   matching
summer's sky sinking into
reflecting water
and
your lips
(soft as a loved cotton shirt)   met mine
in a citrusy-june kiss

unlike any other season.

_____

I am from the Bay Area, California and have been writing poetry since the late 90s. I also enjoy drawing, reading and baking. Allpoetry.com/forgotten_dream

[Nancy Jackson]

Hope Looks to the Future, and Sings

via dolorosa, o hidden way
roll back your stone of death, the tomb of day
...and sing

spring's blush, your buds shout aloud for strength
hold on amid the raging pebble flood
that seeks to sweep away your rich, dark soil
...and sing

blossom's grit, fighting well to labor's end
at twilight's glow you will re-seed again
though biting beetles sting your glossy leaves
and petals drift in breezes to the lea
...and sing

battered blooms, bruised from seed to blossom's tome
the Grower opened earth's most sacred tomb
rise up and joy, you made it to the day
when summer's heat brings shade under the clay
...and sing

winter's chill, cloak well where seedlings pale lay
for spring will follow bitter cold again
seize hope among the stones beneath your stems
...and sing

o via dolorosa, hidden way
roll back your stone to life, the light of day
...and sing!

Nancy Jackson grew up by the ocean but now lives in a valley near the Smoky Mountains. Nature and life experiences frame her poetry and give voice to her spiritual life and healing journey. Allpoetry.com/Nancy_daisygirl

[Lorrie West]

The beautiful farm

There nothing like home especially when its
A beautiful country farm house with green
Trees and pond in the front yard and beautiful
In autumn orange yellow red leaves shining
Old farm house that sit back in the hills red old
Big barn that sit beside it very much a country
Setting green grass that goes forever in the hills
A place like grandma and grandpa use to have
A porch swing and a lot of sun light beauty

_____

My name is Lorrie Ann McConnell-west I write poetry for fun
I've been writing for years now started in my twenties I'm fifty
five years old I have three children which have grown I live in
Michigan Allpoetry.com/lorrie_west

[Terence O'Leary]

War is a War Crime

Once wars were fought with sticks and stones,
flogged foreign flesh and battered bones,
thus conquered lands, defended thrones –
though god forbids, the crowd condones.

The souls assailed by hordes, beset
by battle-axe and bayonet,
braved blades bedecked with blood still wet,
left bodies skewered en brochette,
their lives erased with no regret.

The mad machine's now mechanized,
torment and torture legalized,
blind barbarism globalized
and deeds of demons sanitized.

Each rival's right (just choose a side)
engaged in holy homicide
in view of gods diversified –
fete Cain committing fratricide!

Yes chieftains clash (well hid behind
combatants and the realms they've mined)
while powers, business so entwined
(enmeshed in intrigues, well enshrined)
knit twisted threads, ensnare mankind.

Big Bertha boomed in days of yore –
now ten foot tanks spit spikes of Thor
and mortar shells, like raindrops, pour
upon the plains of Nevermore.

Above, a Drone that terrifies –
a button's pushed, a missile flies
to rip apart, to vaporize
(defending life, they fantasize).

In battlefields where kids once played,
the grumble of a hand grenade
is drowned in claps of cannonade
applauding proud the palisade
where charnel chunks of men lie flayed.

Somewhere a sniper's bullet flies,
somewhere a voiceless victim dies,
somewhere a famished orphan cries
while weapons warble lullabies.

The bunker busters burst the sides
of bulwarks where a folk resides
and innocence in darkness hides –
the die is cast, but who decides?

Strew cluster bombs and barrels too,
(crude critters in the wartime zoo),
to shred more souls than hitherto –
choose death en masse, avoid the queue!

Mean mercenaries hack and maim,
do beastly things that none will name –

well-paid for such, they feel no shame,
like creatures crippled, morally lame.

Dismembered victims everywhere,
most, non-combatants, unaware –
a sole survivor, solitaire,
unfolds her hands, too late for prayer.

Adorned in dirt, a baby cries
with gaping mouth and bleeding eyes,
engulfed in death that money buys –
proud venture vultures view their prize.

It's raining blood and teardrops spill,
enough to drown the daffodil
that withered in the mourning chill –
who was it said 'thou shalt not kill'?

The media's impervious
to truth – they're ever devious,
find every question dangerous,
all scrutiny hence treasonous.

Through eyes lit up like rosy sores,
embedded scribes report on wars
with lore to line the cuspidors –
the Fourth Estate? A herd of whores.

When foreign streets smoke, pulverized,
the body counts are minimized
in front page news that's sterilized
and naked truths are sodomized
to paint the slaughter civilized.

The napalm bombs and phosphorus
and ghastly weapons gaseous
(apportioned widely, bounteous)
beget a desert wilderness!

Oh phosphorous... its flame so white,
exploding, falling through the night,
commemorates the Sacred Rite –
and babes in arms, thus blessed, ignite.

But napalm gel burns slow and calm,
may leave behind a blazing palm
(or better yet, a molten mom
inside a hut) in Vietnam.

Cast chlorine, sarin or VX...
a lethal dose (or side effects
like blistered lungs) will serve to vex –
when victory calls, no one objects...

You close your eyes but can't ignore
that body parts and bags of gore
are bursting through extinction's door,
and strewn beyond the ocean's roar
like rotting fish that wash ashore.

More potent than a blunderbuss
our friend the A-bomb has a plus
(though making one is arduous) –
just need to split the nucleus.

What's more, what's left (more copious,
uranium, depleted thus)

can trash a tank with little fuss,
cause natal cankers, cancerous.

The H of hell will bring much more
unhinged conFUSION to the fore
restoring Stone Age life's rapport –
the surest way to tie the score.

These doomsday warheads (dropped or thrown),
ignited, leave the sun outshone –
beneath a mass of melted stone
lies powdered ash, once flesh and bone.

When atoms bake in bombs debased,
vast cities smolder, laid to waste,
some million sinless souls erased –
perhaps, one day, all life effaced.

POSTSCRIPT
Regard the dreary death Arcade
of Armaments (a fruitful trade)
and tally up the millions made
by ghouls that raise a colonnade
of miles of missiles, weapons-grade,
in Armageddon's crazed parade,
and hide behind a masquerade
of lollipops and lemonade
while planning new each escapade
for sending armies to invade
and loot far oilfields, unafraid
of misery and grief parlayed
until our final days cascade

into a hell no more delayed
by happenstance or luck outplayed
that leaves society decayed,
bombarded with a fusillade
of lies upheld and truth betrayed
by pundits in the shifting shade,
with crises of the world clichéd
and sung in solemn serenade
by journalistic hacks that preyed
on wide-eyed folk in sham charade
that lulls to sleep (with eyelids weighed
by tiny tears that disobeyed
and strayed beyond the barricade)
and bathes the modern-day crusade
of war in cheers and accolade.

The bottom line? Just profits paid
for deadly sins that god forbade...

Retired, enjoys sitting in the garden with some tean and a piece of
pie thinking about the word and life and all that, trying to get
inspired. Allpoetry.com/loquaciousicity

[Andrew Stull]

Looks Like Rain

knuckles too polite to knock
blood pooling at the bone
smiles keeping secrets beneath sandcastles
an insignificant child searching for

home.

fingertips skimming an ocean's lips
sailing away, someplace far
fuck the anchor and pass the sleep
drinking from the bottle of good rum

woozy eyes falling in line
such polite sheep.

may the lighthouse crack and crumble
may my boat ever painted in gasoline
kiss the burning flame of my lucky cigarette

as my eyes melt into my skull
where nightmares are birthed.

looks like rain today.

Andrew Stull is an aspiring novelist and poet from Clarksburg, WV. He uses poetry to help him cope with bipolar disorder and is a mental health advocate. He loves ginger ale and watching rainstorms. Allpoetry.com/Andrew_Stull

[Marta Green]

The Violets

wild dark purple violets in a lush green garden
satiny petals fragrant in a valley of Arden
uniquely beautiful without restraint
almost holy, you are miraculous like a saint

picked at the peak of maturity
a boundless masterpiece of purity
handled with gentle care
so vibrant in the sun, scattering light without a care

putting the velvety flowers in this religious place
intricately patterned, a faceted diamond vase
while bubbling water fill like liquid essence
pale yellow sun beams reflect luminescence

as a centerpiece on the kitchen table
lilac china is spaced evenly, symmetry enabled
viewing these beauties before their mortally timed end
in prayer, life and death do blend

———————————

Marta Green is from the state of Texas where she lives with her husband and son. She has a passion for writing poetry and short stories, her family, and animals. Allpoetry.com/Marta_Green

[Joanna Hixenbaugh]

I Know

I know come spring your ship will sail
and I standing on a worn deck
and will turn my collar up against the
torrent smile bravely but right now
it's winter and I welcome each frost
because I know the sea still lies frozen
I will light the hearth coercing forth warmth
one more night flame flicker across our
brown and blue eyes dance in shadow
across our cheeks and noses keep us huddled
but together exhausted by too much conversation.
Please let me sail to you so I may see
your smile once more!

———————————

I wrote it so many years ago after I lost my best, he was always
saying girl better put your poetry first just remember me for when
your some big hot shot. Allpoetry.com/Shadowbear0608

[Nancy Lee Armstrong]

Four Seasons of the Year

Spring has come, a red robin is now in sight
early morning sun is shining bold and bright
crocus, iris's, daffodils, lilies are all in bloom
colorful butterflies break out of their cocoon

Summer is the hottest time of the season
"for" change of climate there is a reason
walk along the beach enjoy the sunshine
go touring, golfing and fulfilling your dream

Fall days turn into a cool summer breeze
the wind carries brown leaves on the trees
as they fall on the ground leaves lay bare
nature is changing into colors everywhere

Winter snow falls quietly during the night
It covers up all the houses to snowy white
the children build a snowman on the lawn
temperature lowered now they are all gone

All of the seasons only come once a year
spring is alive robins singing lots of cheer
summertime is to have fun enjoy our life
fall is for gathering of harvest and reaping,
winter is Christmas time for love and giving.

My husband David and I reside in Pulaski Virginia. We have one son, Jeff who owns a business company. I am an inspired writer and I am a published author. My book is on Amazon, Most Precious Gift.

Allpoetry.com/Nanarm45

[Stan Holliday]

Where I'll Be

Should you think to look for me
some day after I have gone
the grave is not where I shall be,
of that you can depend upon.

Why would you hope I would be bound
to bones and desiccated flesh
moldering in the cold dark ground
where the winds never blow fresh?

Look for me in the sunset
at the end of a cold winter day
when the moon has not quite risen yet
to announce the end of day.

Or look about in early morn
as the sun wipes sleep from glowing eye
just as the day is being born.
Listen hard, I'll be nearby.

Anywhere the trees grow tall
and whippoorwills repeat their name;
where people seldom walk at all
and rolling hills are filled with game.

Hear me whisper through the wind,
smell muscadines upon my breath.
My lack of life won't be my end,
I'll still be around after my death.

———————————

Born in Memphis then lived from coast to coast as his father was
in the navy. Finally stopped in south Carolina when he retired
back to where he was raised. Attended Clemson University.
Allpoetry.com/Stan_Holliday

[Brady S Bowen]

The Bird Queen

The gentle touch of fingertips
On the outside of my arm
As the sun crawls over the windowsill
Plasmatic molasses
Lighting our togetherness
In the chilled predawn of possibility
That lovers waste on pleasures

Her whispers invade, like auditory amphibious
Soldiers; this beach is mine
They cry, in porcelain fragility
But although she is like the daisy
Her petals are razors, whetted by trial
But they are petals still

I miss the curve of her ankle
the Erotic geometry
Eyes of Tenerife, ethereal
Spun gold threads hang;
A crown.

––––––––––––––

Brady resides close to family in Youngsville, Louisiana. His Celtic roots, rollicking Cajun culture, love and loss have left an indelible mark on his writing and his heart. For The Bird Queen. Allpoetry.com/Brady_Bowen

[Chris Paul Adamson]

tundra

in the e.e. cummings style

a tundra once known
the grassy haze grand
and seeds blown

to a new land
(i saw you the chaos and)
of rabid carbineers
(can your eyes turn to me)
a barrage here and sobs
howling, things whooshing past

their voices carry
from time to time from past now
the same hazy seeds
(you smiled I saw the necks curve)
not dormant they slowly wake

some crying through a cold winter bled
(a heartbeat missed, you smiled twice eyes glowing)
the square is prekrasnyy or red
west and east the crimson grasslands grow
(if i walk, can we touch the closer)
are the dead left with a hero speech
voices and unions an aching

(reach out to the tundra grows)
i ve got you wind and tundra
(and true forever)

From a regional town in N.S.W Australia. Where the river floods and the sun bakes, then the fires burn. It's really quite a lovely place. And poetry, and learning.

Allpoetry.com/Christopher5

[Jonathan Copic]

Inferno

Brimming with potential,
glass ceilings were destined to break.
She moved with the winds of change.
Men rounded their heads to her passing,
inconceivable was the road that lay ahead.
Her essence burned,
the world was putty in her hands.
Avant-garde was she.
Afraid not of what lied ahead
lustful embers burned
deep and true within her.
Scorching the insipid trails
left
by her predecessors,
cultivating curiosity within a seduced populace.
She stood in solitaire,
but they revered together;
for she was sacred.

_____

From Arkansas, I write to express thoughts and feelings I struggle
to verbalize; it has given me a great outlet for growth.
Allpoetry.com/copic

[Kimberley Baker]
Moonless Night

Ebony blankets the night sky
after chasing the velvet sunset away.
As the inky dark bled over the purple and pink
they played out the end of day

Stars peek through tiny pinholes
causing ripples to sparkle and glow
Ocean dancing with the pull of tides
as the waves gently ebb and flow

Salty onyx water caresses the sand
at the edge of the waters reach
Marine creatures along for the ride
trying not to be left on the beach

———————————

I am a new grandmother and it has really changed my perspective
on a lot of things. Pl I write poetry to let out my overwhelming
feelings. I want to make others feel something.
Allpoetry.com/Kimberley_Baker

[Shelly Nichols]

Climbing the walls

Magic dancing in the sunlight...
Your ghost keeps climbing the walls.
I'm melting somewhere near the sand dunes
Where the river flows through.
Still another tequila sunrise,
when I think of you.

───────────────

California is my home..
But my heart breathes easily in Arizona.
I write from my dreams..
I write about people I dearly love..
I write to keep my heart peaceful..
I write to entertain poetic genius.

Allpoetry.com/Shelly_Nichols

[Lorri Ventura]

Barn Spider

Pre-dawn moonbeams kiss her web
As she waits, poised to pounce
When a moth flutters haplessly
Toward her gossamer labyrinth.

Her black and amber body
Clings, motionless, to her cat's cradle,
Which shimmers in one corner of a hayloft window.

Her barnyard companions
Nicker, stomp, snort, and crow,
Restlessly signaling their hunger,
Eagerness for the sun to rise,
And need for acknowledgment.

The barn spider, though, knows
That no one will come to feed, groom,
Or greet her.
Serenely she waits for her intricate handiwork
To ensnare her meal.

A model of humility and self-sufficiency,
The arachnid shows us
That hard work and perseverance,
Often unnoticed,

Bring fulfillment

Lorri Ventura is a retired special education administrator living in Massachusetts. Her writing has been featured in a number of anthologies. Allpoetry.com/Lorri_Ventura

hard truths

The lost cause of the confederacy
I'm no lost cause In tense moments on neutral grounds

This is the messy work of reckoning

TriBeCa is new to you and neutral ground to me
MEDITATION 🧘 is THE real 👧 FILM NOIR
SOJOURNER TRUTH DISSECTS LIES IN PASSION, film
noir is where now? In The antebellum south, if your public
broadcasting system is accompanied by Helen hunt it's intensely
festive lol

They call that a movie its title is deep impact —> I can't have that
either so instead I proud to say I went to Milton in 2003 the year
the filmmaker CJ huNt graduated, his new documentary is about
neo confederates
He has bravado he isn't Helens son but he is confident and has
critical acclaim so the lines we draw maybe intersectional.

One and two and three things are now the same they running
close to the ostrich in the race to win the championship for who
stole my heart and broke it first with their tsunami 🌊 of
neoclassical 🎭 on races away from things we can't escape.

Contesta me Dios por favor. Si hacia Dios bueno porque no
puedo tener lo bueno y son tristeza y pena en el mundo toda vía.
Why can't the ostrich fly? She si is heavy and the dodo 🐦 extinct ?
No se when we will peder this bird to extinction but let's save the

flightless bottom-heavy birds and Rubénesque and squalid this is my request. Thanks dare to love you mama too.

Why do we think we know the weary 😮 🗩, and where or where the stories are going, western civilizations, stores, Wes cravens film of reconciliations, why do we think we know the ending or the journey of the protagonist !

When your heart is broken
You're wonton and you will not go but you will go when pushed

You wouldn't go before because your gut said you're stuck here. But get your head out the mud Amanda, your heart is not tarred and feathers ▯,

Girls you are like my ancestor the ostrich and I say you can lift your broken heart out the LA BREA TAR PITS.

And maybe you lift your head again but your wings can't fly and you won't soar, but surely the ostrich you are will run toward the evil that broke your aorta and rush it to An ER FOR ITS BUCUSPID VALve.

Highly rich history birds have, they are not the lost cause of the confederacy nor of history or of plumages. Ruffle our feathers and we rise again. And peck back. I learned that in drama at Milton. Academy. Thanks mr. Peck. lol haha

New beginnings remove the monumental ideology that civil is end of water.

———————————————

I'm from New York , New York. I write poetry because it gives me life. I'm a scientist and teacher by trade but I really enjoy spoken word and I studied English heavily in high school and college. Allpoetry.com/Persephone8

[Lorri Ventura]

The Tin Dollhouse

Life never changes
Inside the tin dollhouse.
Mommy stands in the kitchen,
Eternally offering lunchboxes
To her two smiling children,
Permanently clad in their best school clothes.
She does not have to fear
That her beloved babies
Will be shot in their classrooms.

Daddy poses forever
On the kelly green metal lawn,
Attached to the hose he aims
At the ever-blooming zinnias
Painted along the house's side.
He does not worry that unrestrained
Expulsion of pollutants
Will contaminate his garden,
The unending stream of water,
Gushing from his hose,
Or the air he breathes.

A plastic woman walks her silicone dog
Past the tin dollhouse
With no concerns that a government
Will steal her reproductive rights,

Persecute her for the color of her skin,
For whom she loves,
Or how she worships.

Leaning in a doorway
Beyond the tin dollhouse
A mother gazes at her little girl,
Crouched on the floor,
Peering into each miniature room.
She sighs softly
And wishes her daughter's world were as safe and just
As the one embodied by her toy.

Lorri Ventura is a retired special education administrator living in Massachusetts. Her writing has been featured in a number of publications. She has won two Moon Prizes for her poetry. Allpoetry.com/Lorri_Ventura

[J.G Pollard]

rOy of the rainbow

The snapping bitterness of orange juice in the mornings
along with the fuzzy, calm layer of sunshine
orange, speaks louder than all
known for it's neon attributes
in roller rinks and glowsticks
unpleasant to some
a warm hug to the rest
it is more of what bears the fruit
but a spectrum of ambience to our eyes
it beams to all and sticks in our brain
like traffic cones that reek of solitude
and of little leagues to pros
orange, seeks revenge
and is bitter to the end

J.G.Pollard lives in the suburbs of Kansas City, where sports and music triumphs. They write on any day of any kind, especially in certain moods. Rainy days give extra inspiration and comfy vibes. Allpoetry.com/JoplinJay

[Stephen Puls]

Fire on The Border

Fire is coming over the border
Russians are coming with the pain
There is chaos and mass disorder
The end is coming quickly for Ukraine
Tanks and soldiers bearing many guns
Are making a military change
Bullets and bombs by the metric ton
Assures and uneven fire exchange
Children screaming in the fog of war
Mother's scrambling for a safe haven
The Ukrainians have their hell in store
Revenge is what the Russians are craving
Russian Rockets screaming their deadly cries
War machines rumbling down the highway
The Beast wants it all without compromise
Frightened families cower in the subways
The world can only sit with eyes of rage
As the innocent die for Putins greed
This leader has freed his dogs from their cage
Putin is taking what he has decreed

My writing is my therapy. I was an E.M.T. For many years and
have some anxiety type issues. Poetry gives my mind peace. I am
from Tewksbury, Ma. Allpoetry.com/Stephen2

[Ronald Dereaux]

Muse searching

Running across green fields
and over loose sand
I'll retrace the paths
that have been lost
in search for your hand

Climbing tall trees
while floating on air
looking forward
to the far horizon,
usually you are there

Memorizing the stars
enjoying the embrace
of the phosphorus moon
my muse waiting patiently
for syncing with me in tune

—————————

Dereaux is from the Low Lands and here at AP I try to put my
thoughts about whatever comes to mind to a written work. In my
spare time I try to do the same ;) Allpoetry.com/Dereaux

[Stephen Hollins]

Neruda's footprints

dead woman, lend me your spine
that I may never abandon the poor
or bend a knee to dictators' hooves
running roughshod to blacken blacks

dead woman, lend me your arm
to share your joy and sorrows weight
dead woman, kiss this heartbeat
so I may warm the hearts of all mankind

my feet to print your shadow in the snow
and my hands to lift up the dead
like a child's stick and leaf boat
rocking through rivers boulders
roaring victory at the sea

to carry brothers, sisters, and children
in wooden chests rocking in loves ocean
for what is life but a light shining inside
that we waking blind cannot see
or extinguish

in the silvery frost of moon's breath
your feet call me
to step upon darkest mountains

towards that soft place called sleep
but I must go on, living

_____

I live on beautiful Waiheke Island in New Zealand. I specialize in Improv for theatre, dance, clown, and mime, teaching adults to become more playful, building, and being a dad.
Allpoetry.com/Stephen_Hollins

[Douglas Smith]

Surf the Night

Orange, purple, fluorescent and yellow
From the bow, beautiful pew

Black, blue, hurtle, blazing deep wake
Break, crash, now currently awake

Splash, blast, thrash, the moon searches sunrise
Wait, outlast, hope, soon ending

Wrap, slap, lapse, endured, now blithe
Shake erased, new view, increase breathing

———————————

I am trusting, ever loving, to the point of blindness.

Might be a crime thus, mindless love until you find one that
reminds us you deserve more.

Much. A reminding crux, you're entitled to such.
Allpoetry.com/Djgs117

[Nigel Bangert]

taking the underground

so the day is going well
which is never a good sign
time ticking past somnambulantly
inducing a soporific state
I find hard to shake
with rocking carriages
as I traverse to my travail
through millennia of archaeology
passing long extinct dinosaurs
turning magically to crude oil
Roman armies with Gladius drawn
ready for action two thousand
years on, still trying to conquer
the unconquerable realm
then an eco-warrior
of shabby description
yells my carbon footprint
is an abominable erection
it's an electric train I holler
how much greener can I be fella
the Romans are looking friendlier
by the minute they only wanted
my freedom not justification of existence
the soporific state abates

the modern world is against me
now I'm running late

_____

I am a van driver from Essex, where I live with my wife and three
grown up children. I write and take pictures for my own
amusement, though I do sell my images and I have been
published a few times. Allpoetry.com/Nigdaw

[Paulette Gordon]

Roman Angels

I spent a time
in line
But magic was mine

Roman angels
smoky air
Chaining bangles
long hair

Dangerous buses
Fighting words
Warm lap
Perfect fit
Theater across the street
Orgasms in the flat
Buy stock in Trojan

Il bacio
at the show
Please never go

Airport, airplane
reaching out
Write, explain
even shout

Italian rings
Joy it brings
7pm, really? 7pm
Wow, that's just them
Those Italians
Those Roman angels
From the nightclub

———————————

Hi! I'm a wife and mama in California. Since my girlhood I have
written skits, short stories + poems. My first love was the stage
though. Now it is poetry. Glad to be part of this community.
Allpoetry.com/Flying_Elephant

[Carla Horne]

becoming e.e. cummings

when was to not ask
    find where whirling washing water
  keep alliteration with alligator
    inventing vocabulario
      mi amigo where has gone to come back
the question begged how
    return to sleep not for eyes wide shut
      hola to what degree

adverbs school not here just time   to help   tear not lest fear all

synapses run haywire where are the waves.   ocean floor taking
more

salt wave let the how find the when
    where   will come on its own

like a werewolf in not light   change not seeing
    what is coming
answers to a pronoun hostage to the noun
    cummings
    liked
    balloons

I have always adored reading and writing poetry. Since I have retired from teaching, I have enjoyed Allpoetry.com and the wonderful people here. Allpoetry.com/Crafty_Mermaid

[Katherine Stachurski]

naranja.

the texture under my fingertips
connects to a wet tongue
through my nerves
as anticipation for the first bite ascends

a quick stab of nails
through a thickened flesh
follows a tender pull and peel

will you be sweet?
or perhaps a little too sour for my taste...

...I just hope this time I got a ripe one

———————————

Katherine was born in Southern California. Writing began as an escape from trauma and anxiety in her youth. What was once a crutch is now a delightful hobby she shares with her growing family. Allpoetry.com/wildflower.

[Lisa F. Raines]

The Horrors of War

Do you see the dead women
on the side of the road?
Do you know what war is?

Can you see the dead men,
burned and blackened?
Do you know what war is?

There are towns of rubble, and
cities filled with death.
Do you know what war is?

Where children played,
they now lay dead.

This is what war is—
it always has been.

———————

AlisRamie is from North Carolina, USA.
Interests include: philosophy, history, international relations,
poetry, art, design, jazz, funk rock, and some good old soul.
Allpoetry.com/AlisRamie

[Laura Sanders.]

Black

He stalks in and out of the shadows
hides behind the pillars
prowls on velveteen toes.....
crouches then transforms,
man to Feline
in a split second....silent paws.

The silhouettes hide his form-
his shape.
Suddenly he springs
at lightning speed.....
Puma at dusk.
A flash of claws
whiskers, and THOSE eyes.....
Only the darkness knows
what he has left behind, then.... sighs....

Waiting behind a dust-cart
then a suburban tree,
only light bathes the mess,
He refuses to flee.....
On into a park,
following a twisted path,
unhurried steps,
a grim end for that black man,
the noise had echoed out

piercing the silence,
in a dark park,
in a dark town,
in a dark place.....

I live in a beautiful part of the country, England and take inspiration from observing nature, people and animals.I enjoy writing all sorts of poetry . Allpoetry.com/Laura_Sanders.

[Marta Green]

Matriarch Of The Family

crinkly, outlined brown eyes
look deeply into mine
crepe white skin shimmers
a pale yellow cashmere blanket
keeps fragile shoulders warm

she speaks with a wavering voice
her mind, razor sharp but her body is failing
cancer has you like a tail on a kite
wheelchairs huddled like a herd of cows
in an assisted living ward
watching a show, "Judge Judy"

as if in slow motion, I see you Grammy
walking quickly to your side
kissing cheeks so delicate like tissue paper
I take your arthritic misshapen blue veined hands
delicately into mine, a smile blossoms like a pink rose on your lips
showing some missing teeth

pushing your wheelchair to a nook, you say excitedly
"So what's new?" as I spill the gossip of the family
my young step daughter is pregnant at the tender age of eighteen
yes, my parents are well like a pristine, Rembrandt
peaceful, cohesive, at one with each other
haven't heard from my brother, he is mad at us for moving away

kept in touch with childhood friends
still laughing like hyena's at perceived humor

conversation turns towards me
"Have you met anyone?"
"So what's he like."
"Do you think you'll marry him?"
"I would love to see more babies!"
this coming from a woman who adores children, especially babies
smiling a bitter sweet smile, I assure that "maybe, some day."

———————————

Marta Green is from the state of Texas, about an hour from the gulf coast. She loves writing poetry and short stories. Her husband and family are some of her greatest supporters! Allpoetry.com/Marta_Green

Personification of Evil

Peering into their neighbors' eyes,
The two rough-necked males gleaned no surprise,
From the pasture,
To the garden,
Some hearts would break,
Some hearts would harden,
Two democratic figures stood,
Behind the fence just like they should,
Trying to get the golden geese,
So that they might bear Golden Fleece,
Chicklets were there to be protected,
Not to be maimed or to be neglected,
The fence stood up so firm and strong,
"Build the Wall!" We sang along.
Apparently, that was enough,
It kept them out despite their gruff,
No matter how scary or tough,
Those democrats could not touch the stuff,
The golden geese that laid gold eggs,
Hatched pretty chicks with tiny legs,
Roamed, and played, and prayed all day,
Those damned donkeys just wanted their way.
So they stood beside the wall,
Although it was not big or tall,
It kept them sitting there at bay,

With no sign reading, "GO AWAY!"
So the Democrats would stay.

Author's Notes: Word Count 160
Tags: Politics, Animal Farm, 2020

Glenn Folkes got his graduate degree from the University of
North Texas. He still writes poetry and music.
Allpoetry.com/Barkdream69

[Brady S Bowen]

Short Street

There is a tiny kingdom
in my tiny town
diminutive Cajun emirate
a principality of shade

its muraled bricks ablaze
rainbow-hued paper dream cars
you reveal it to mother
like its new every morning

mama that's a trans am
the mullet-man is rude
he never even looks at me
lost in thought; discourteous

a climate-controlled corridor
a secret-September
for the flowing moment
of darkened transitory vacation

———————————

Brady resides close to family in Youngsville, Louisiana. His Celtic roots, rollicking Cajun culture, love and loss have left an indelible mark on his writing and his heart. For The Bird Queen. Allpoetry.com/Brady_Bowen

[Stacey Guenther]

Space

vacuous space clouds

floating in the universe -

cosmic dust and gas

_____

I'm from Indiana. I'm an artist and I've recently decided to write
poetry. I'm starting with Haiku, Senryu, and Tanka.
Allpoetry.com/ArtistEnchantingFox

[Keith Pailthorp]

ole maam river

oh lawn gandsuffering river
how often have
the callous hands of men
made bold to divert and/or
entertain you
to bind and/or
bend your means to their prurient ends/or
how miserably have the uncivil
engineers failed to
reengineer your wildness into a placid lake
how mutely have you
mutilated their moot question
with a beggared prior question
and how surely have you restored
to your birth mother
the life-giving water that was ever hers alone?

Keith Pailthorp is a former radiation physics researcher at Battelle
Northwest Laboratory (Hanford) and latter-day planner for
several state agencies that coordinate higher education. He is
retired. Allpoetry.com/Keith_Pailthorp

[Paul Goetzinger]

Eclipse

The Moon
Waxes crimson
In darkest hours
A ballet enrobed
Disappearing
Into earth's shadow
A coppery, reddish glow
Rising

As wolves' howl outside villages
Children stir from sleep
To view Apollo's painting
In dust and smoke
Star gazers stare upwards
Striking a profile
While night owls hunt
In fading light

Paul Goetzinger is a freelance writer and educator from Des Moines, Washington. He has written articles for magazines and other publications for the past 18 years.
Allpoetry.com/Paul_Goetzinger

[Marcy Clark]

Disappearing

His world has shifted
from the ordinary
to a poorly lit path

He knows the way home on a brisk autumn morning
or thinks he does
until a neighbor opens the front door

and points back up the lane
to our cottage

I take this slow journey with him
those slippery summer months of deception
when nothing is out of place

conversations each day are playful
and include the dog
or memories of the boys

then that shift
that shivery winter freeze
when he asks where they are
and I lie

Writing poetry has become my passion, my time machine fueled with both sad and wonderful memories that keep my loved ones near
Allpoetry.com/Grandmakittyfl

[Douglas Smith]

Hearts Tied Together

Bound up by your trust
Found
Forced
Unforced
Lust

Chained down by your face
Eyes
Describe
Demand
My place

Roped in by your body
Soft
Aloft
Pressing
My troth

Surrounded by your thighs
Cushioning
Squeezing
Begging
My all

Encompassed by your arms
Triumphant

Non-reluctance
Crumpling
Please, more

Commanded by your fire
Burning
Warning
Inviting
Warming

Now it's my turn.

I am trusting, ever loving, to the point of blindness.

Might be a crime thus, mindless love until you find one that reminds us you deserve more.

Much. A reminding crux, you're entitled to such.
Allpoetry.com/Djgs117

[Samuel K. Williams III MD CPG]
Thick poem

Is this a poem that is as thick as you?
Are these lines bigger than those chocolately big-thighs?
Are the verses, stanzas and lines as fine
As you appear in your ruddiness so supple in my view?
Would a kiss of these syllables be as soft as your lips
Chocolate fe is a understatement in this poetic expression
The brown skin that covers you like a golden ocean
Is a better reflection of the sweet depth of seas and the fishes that
swim inside of your garden
On a bright sun-shiny day a palleta would cannot replace
The chilly beauty of your face which is more of a sweet treat
Than all the brown sugar in the syrupy sweets

———————————

41 year old physician and father of 3 children living in Albany, Georgia. I currently practice tele-health and plan on publishing my entire poetry collection within a year.
Allpoetry.com/The_Thoughtsider

[Robert W. Hancock]

The Fisherman

The north wind cut into the fisherman's face
as slowly he moved toward the place
where late season catches might be big;
big enough perhaps to meet his need.

His thoughts were troubled by luck run dry;
Wiping his eyes he wondered why
fate had crushed such hopes before
bringing him now to desperation's door.

The nets were ready, the time was then
to pull his nets against the wind,
but in the end he failed again;
returning home poorer than before.

Robert W. Hancock is a native of Harkers Island, NC, where he
lives with his wife of 66 years, Nola. He served in the U.S. Coast
Guard from 1955 to 1975, when he retired as a Chief Boatswain's
Mate. Allpoetry.com/Bill_Hancock3

[Jim Beitman]

The kitties took over the craft room

The kitties took over the craft room
And the puppy decided to join
They tugged and hugged the fabric and yarn
While spilling the baskets
But doing no harm
Making a mess was nothing new
It's one of the funniest things they do
Being creative with craft supplies
Bonded them together
Sharing high fives
Celebrating their nine lives
All the energy tuckered them out
As they did confess
A nap topped off the fun
Curled up in the mess

I am an artist living in Noblesville Indiana. Writing is a great media that helps distill my feelings, thoughts, and experiences. It is always a great thrill to be included in an Allpoetry anthology! Allpoetry.com/Beitmanjim

[Douglas Smith]

Our Hearts

Deep   Free
Craft blast   And brash
Outlast hash   My bombast
An everlasting yes ma'am
Heal thee outclassing
So deeply drastic
Crash fantastic
No tragic
We

I am trusting, ever loving, to the point of blindness. Might be a
crime thus, mindless love until you find one that reminds us you
deserve more. Much. A reminding crux, you're entitled to such.
Allpoetry.com/Djgs117

[Douglas Smith]

Why shouldn't I believe?

Why should I believe
That He is waiting for me?
Why focus emotions
Away from His accomplishing?
Why think of His heart not beating
When, in mind, I can see
His greatest endeavor...
Me.

Why should I focus
On Her eternal compliance?
Why believe what She believes?
Why sigh at Her non-existent crying?
She's a bridge never fallen.

Why shouldn't I focus
On His selfless sacrifices?
Why disrespect His memory
Of His defiance of stolen contrivance?

Why shouldn't I focus
On Her selfless love?
Why decry Her unabated
Unnecessary
Irresistible
Bliss, and all.

Keep your Diety
To yourself
I have my own
To worship two.
Mi propio Dios y Diosa.

I am trusting, ever loving, to the point of blindness. Might be a crime thus, mindless love until you find one that reminds us you deserve more. Much. A reminding crux, you're entitled to such.
Allpoetry.com/Djgs117

[Deadra Willis]

Tragedy

It's the emptiness,
the void,
being stared back at
by the abyss...

Like bulging eyes,
vacant of any compassion
or mercy,
intent upon you -
upon damaging you.

Tracking you through
time and space,
piercing any impediment
you put in the way,
dissolving it like a mist.

You watch
with no eyelids,
as its mental fingers
like jagged shards, jab
and hook and pull
your brain
and shred it into ribbons.

And you,
struck dumb and ineffectual
in your own defense,

as in your dreams of frustration
and impotence,
where you try to throw a punch
but your wrist goes limp,
you try to fly
but you can't concentrate
to get off the ground.

And nothing else is only
what it seems to be,
as it masks itself as other,
camouflages its true nature
and intent,
disguising itself
as harmless.

The entire background begins to morph
and change and undulate,
dripping the colors of reality away
to reveal the pitch,
the something more than dark
that was always hiding
...behind everything.

———————————

Phoenix Aradia wears a gossamer nom de plume, so that she may
be otherwise bare on these white sheets of paper...and computer
screens. Mother to a Cub Scout named Fox, and owner of a little
zoo. Allpoetry.com/Phoenix_Aradia

[Victoria Pearson]

I Saw Them All

I took a walk this morning,
the Sun was high, the soft
winds slightly stirring,

My steps they led along the way,
no choice I had no say.

I found myself atop a mountain high,
with people down below, many
were in that Valley, but to
me they seemed the same.

Though some had skins of copper brown,
other's pure fine porcelain,
with shades from light to dark...yet,

I loved the took of all their eyes, so many colors seen,
yes, some were blue, other's brown, one with hazel
too, lovely yes to see, I even saw a shade of
greenish blue...Could that have even been you!

Each had nose that they could use, as
I myself can do, with ears that
matched my very own, to hear with as I can.

They all had mouths, yes I have one too,
to speak, or not, like me, you see,
the world is just that way.

Forget, some do, that all were formed by our,
own loving God, though different looks,
one from another, each one is still His child,

There is no difference deep inside, but that's
for us to see, so on a morning clear, yes
warm, come take a walk with me.

Let's look right down that Valley found,
you'll see the same things too!

_____

I have been writing poetry for many years, and enjoy the
Traditional forms, as well as Free Verse, and Prose Poetry...
Allpoetry.com/my3doggies

[Douglas Smith]

We Ride The Wave

My brain
a gas tank
Forward focusing
it drives
straight at it
no looking back
until it runs out

That's what's been happening
lately,
I've been veering
towards whatever
the first
traumatic
or ridiculous
thoughts hit
my memories
it leads
without me
seeing
a way up
from down.

It's a double edge sword,
it leads my mind
like blinders

and I run
down that track
A subversive attack

It happened last night
where I was a different person
and you felt
rightfully
offended
because I had a one-track mind

But you rode
That wave
On my board
Because you know
My soul

—————————————

My brain is this way because we all are at some point at least once.
But she willingly surfs my interpolations. And, reciprocally, I
willingly swim to her wake of trepidations. We are we,
partnership. Allpoetry.com/Djgs117

The Anthropomorphic Personification of

Extreme Vindictive Altruism And

Cannibalism's Love-Child

"And so, a peculiar personification of cannibalism comes into being, as violence begets new hunger."

As far as births go, mine was fast
I'd arrived in but one hour
Few might've been a bit quicker
Fewer with dice like mine cast
When I occurred, the world changed
"The Feasting Hour", I was named

My conception rooted in death
And perpetual massacre
Retribution, kill the killers!
Through that, I took my first breath
They'd thought they did themselves good
Turning the feeders into food

Modern media; movies, books
Hosting those that share my same tastes
Portray us as *antagonists*!
Spitting and giving us strange looks

I swear, they're obsessed with us
And serving us, "Karmic Justice"

In my case, that objective's null
I slouched *forth* from that bloody womb!
Slithered *forth* from that violent cock!
Jumped from gnashing, *howling* skulls!
So, how could *I* be subdued
By the "Blood For Blood" attitude?

All it took was just one hour
For me to step into the sun
At the hands of altruistics
Now consumed by *my* power
With *my* house and home in their hearts
This is where the excitement starts

———————————

Pronounced 'Hawsk Tuk-swa'. I am Midwest born. Poetry has &
continues to be an acceptable outlet for many of the things that
take up residence in my mind & what may or may not be
considered a 'soul'. Allpoetry.com/Hawsk

The painting

The paint-less painting,
the brushless paint,
the handless brush,
perfectly depicted

What a surprise!

Ben is from Vancouver, Canada. Writing poetry is the expression of this moment, unfolded and unformed. Allpoetry.com/BenV

[Angela Wunder]
Mother Ocean, Source of all Life

The scent of salt in the air. Sandpipers dancing without a care. The relentless roar of waves hitting the shore. Me, feeling the movement of the beach floor. The ocean, from whence all life came. Totally wild, none shall ever tame. Seashells and jellyfish dotting the beach. Gulls, swooping and diving, do screech. The ocean blessed by the dazzling sun up high; and while watching dolphins breach into the sky, I do sigh. Ah, someday, I'll go back to the coast, to the place I love most. And, again, wade the shores of Mother ocean, source of all life. A place of tranquility, free from needless strife.

––––––––––––

Angela Wunder (Heidicat, pen name) lives near St. Paul, MN with her three cats. When she was younger, she raised two sons and worked as a waitress. Besides writing poems, she likes all forms of art. Allpoetry.com/Heidicat

[Ellen Lovell]

how the flowers grow

beneath the pear tree, I sit and watch
as your trowel digs in the dirt.
again and again.
you point to mounds of earth and tell me what grows there;
pansies, some honeysuckle, a whole patch for snowdrops.
you will not see them for months,
and I do not yet understand why you spend so much time here.
do you not know that you can buy flowers?
mother keeps a vase full, and here I only see the seeds.
but you let me water them,
let me poke the labels into the dirt even though I cannot read
them yet
and I wonder how the flowers will grow when you're gone.

I think of those summers as you drive us up North,
car full of new kitchenware and every piece of clothing I own.
Sinatra sings softly,
windows cracked enough to let a breeze in.
September crept up quickly
as it always does
but you would never guess it, by the purple seas on either side of
us, as deep as they were in July.
I have never liked lavender,
but you find beauty in anything sprouted from the dirt
and so I roll my windows down further as we pass, until the
country air fills the car.

you comment on the beauty of the scent.
my nostrils burn, nose wrinkles,
and you tap along to the music as you drive.

I blame myself, the next year
as I stare at the vase on my windowsill.
I let the flowers wilt
let them sit, dry, in the glass for too long.
the tap was right there
and I let them thirst.
Vision blurred, I toss them out
and dress in blue
hoping that the blooms from the florist will not suffer the same
fate.
they do, of course.
lavender and lilies reducing to dust beside you on the mantlepiece.
they may never know your caring hands,
but at least they get to wilt beside you.

when the snow melted,
I was sure the ground would stay bare,
that the trees would stay empty.
I willed them to still, to stop growing, to stop reaching for the sun
wondering how the earth could bear to turn without you.
the cold suited me,
darkness stopped the sun seeping in,
frost encouraged my hibernation.
then,
snowdrops.
beneath a barren tree.

frozen soil, a tuft of grass,

and snowdrops.

for a moment, I think about ripping them out.

how dare they.

how dare they bloom.

how can they, even

when you are not here to care for them?

but the wind blew,

lifted them up to peek at me,

green hearts on their leaves,

and I faltered.

spring is here,

and somehow, you are not.

I still do not know how the flowers grow without you.

all I know is that they do.

———————————

Ellen, 25, from Birmingham (UK), has been writing since she was a child, flicking between projects and mediums but never putting down the pen for too long. Allpoetry.com/zellora_stwist

[Nigel Bangert]

centuries apart

my wife watches tik tok in bed
sounding like she is trying
to tune in a radio to someone's life
so many voices fading in and out
or maybe a spirit box with a message
from the other side

I'm with Johannes Gutenberg
some 570 years behind
the smell of the print as much
an enjoyment as the words inside
the book I am reading
about his life

we lie
a respectable distance between us
centuries apart

––––––––––––

I am a published poet living in Essex, UK. I have been writing since my teens, it's always been an itch I've needed to scratch. Allpoetry.com/Nigdaw

[Brendan Scott Annandale]

Flame of Life

Oceans of agony, floating away from me,
Hopelessly hatred speaks, only complacently
Creations a spine for our fate that's assigned
And spaces designed to encase the matrix of mind

The land we traverse, expands as the earth
Standing in dirt, handling the mantle of birth
Skys that burn, comprised of cycles learned
Clockwise it turns until our times adjourned

We break and bend to change the trends
Patiently trained to mend our ancient zen,
Comets that dance the night lost in romance
Promise no chance of our profits enhanced

The wolf hides its face, denying its rage
Subsiding climates break residing in place
The winds of fate singing, swing and sway
Kindred faith and a place where kings await

Days are bright, fading to a sustaining night
The flame of life's an abrasive abstaining light

————————————

Brendan Annandale lives in Kingston, Ontario. Interests include
writing, reading, camping, hiking, exercising and swimming.
Writing poetry since the age of 15.
Allpoetry.com/Brendan_Annandal

[S. Libellule]

The Language of Rain

Rain speaks in an ancient tongue
one we learn while we are young
for each pitter-patter whispers
secrets old and deep

Awake or asleep
we hear their origin story
bear our solemn witness
to all the loss it will confess

Whether in sprinkle or downpour
we are willing to hear more
than what is mentioned
what is actually said

Of both the living and the dead
tears shed down through the years
with words spoken true and plain
in the language of the rain

Originally from New England, Libellule currently lives outside of Birmingham, Alabama. Poetic influences include Mary Oliver and Billy Collins. Poems are usually about nature and its awesomeness. Allpoetry.com/Little_Dragonfly

[Nancy Jackson]

A Different Tune

a concrete poem
in the style
of e.e. cummings
also called
visual
and form
poetry

Nancy Jackson grew up by the ocean but now lives in a valley near
the Smoky Mountains. Nature and life experiences frame her
poetry and give voice to her spiritual life and healing journey.
Allpoetry.com/Nancy_daisygirl

[Nick J. Vincelli]

Retrograde Ruminations

I
of
warped words
& soundless mind
out of mindless sight
no(some)where
blurring into
the No-Go Realm
(chasing cunning
cryptic clouds
of thoughtcrimes)

I touch
no man's land
out never
where I'm supposed
to be or
not begin

I am there
not here
catastrophically
contemplating
caricatures
of contorted
mindscapes

I am here or there
out of control
cleverly out of sorts
sorting out
sordid
collusive
clutter

evading
enemies
in the
Dog Days of Delusion
one
dissolving
poem
at a time
(time a at
emit a ta
eat
ate)
composing symphonies of
poignant
collapse
collaps
collap
colla
col
co
c
--
while
f

176

a
l
l
i
n
g
¡FALLiNG!

I am (t)here
heretofore
hermetically
hallucinating
(elucidating)
zephyrs of
hell

I am not
hereoutthere
but in the sorrid
whereness
of concocted
weaponized
words

I am here
seeking
terrifying stardoom
sailing through
the tragicomic
mimetic memes
(tumbling

turbulently
into the
anti-universe)

I send
heat-seeking
missives towards
Austeroid
where
alienated artisans
eat alien
space bats

My purpose
(dis)served
as I seek my
missing muse
from the
musing Minotaur
and a
peaceful OBE
upward
towards the
noosphere

———————————

I'm a librarian and currently reside in North Carolina. I was born
in NYC and also lived in Austin, TX where I graduated from UT-
Austin (BA & MLIS). I've also written fiction and reviews.
Allpoetry.com/J.Tomcatx

[Keith Pailthorp]

Friends and Lovers

The tragedy of Jay Gatsby was not his death
But rather the centrifugal force of his death
Daisy and the cuckold's proper target
Were gone with the wind in a gust of righteous indignation
The scores of moths that had been drawn to Jay's flame
Were not even curious enough to risk attending his funeral
Only the eccentric MacIntosh Man who had crashed in Jay's
library
Was so inept as to make a furtive entrance and exit
In token of his fleeting regard
Jay's exit was as seemingly accidental as his entrance.
And as strangely and hauntingly sad
He was a romantic in a world of pragmatists
Jay Gatsby's shining fifteen minutes of fame
Were as substantial as cotton candy in the rain

Keith Pailthorp is a former radiation physics researcher at
Hanford and a planner for several states' agencies that coordinate
higher education. He and his wife are retired on a pond in Davis,
CA. Allpoetry.com/Keith_Pailthorp

[David Nelson]

And you, my father, my other skin

And you, my father, my other skin
In that sweat of exhaustion
Saw me turn away disbelieving
The end was fast approaching

Lying in that room
Red faced and gasping for breath
Chest heaving, mask slipping
Blasted by fever's heat

The slick ease of cowardice
The excuse the eyes cannot see
Blinded by love's denial
A selfishness supreme

Life's colour bleached out
A new reality to embrace
His numbed fingers fail to grip
The life that's slipped away

But your spirit is not vanquished
It's fused within my heart and bones
My blood, my life, my kin

––––––––––––––––––––

David83 is a newbie to poetry but has always loved writing since a
child. He is retired and shares his experience and sometimes
unorthodox views on life Allpoetry.com/Dylan83

[Sean Cooke]

Enemies of the Board

The queen is left crying as she parts ways with the king.
She knows the end is in sight and lays down for the knight.
The king is sweating as he sways from side to side.

He watches his castles crumble.
He has nowhere to hide.
The knight no longer gallops to the king's aid.
He takes off his shoes the final move has been played.

The bishops in retreat he's no longer with the king.
His heart feels heavy and tarnished with sin.
The king falls to his knees while the enemies close in.
He takes off his crown and stutters the words "you win".

———————————

I am a 32 year old man from northern England, reading and writing poetry is now a satisfying and productive part of my life. I thank my mother and father deeply and all those who read my poetry. Allpoetry.com/Arsenalfan30

[Jim Beitman]

the waves arrive in rhythmic form

the waves arrive in rhythmic form
as regular as a clock
they break on the land
return and re-align
and again massage the sand

I am an artist living in Noblesville Indiana. Writing is a great
media that helps distill my feelings, thoughts, and experiences. It
is always a great thrill to be included in an Allpoetry anthology!
Allpoetry.com/Beitmanjim

[Jason Aaron Davies]

I die too

Withered away beneath me
Like a canvas primed

All the voices echoing
From a landless time

Their spirits roam freely
As the sky burns blue

Reaching out to teach me
That I die too

I was Born in May of 1986. I am from Cincinnati, Ohio. I have
two daughters, one sister and one brother. I enjoy writing,
painting and music. My father passed away December 17th, 2020
and we miss him. Allpoetry.com/JasonAaron86

[Andrew lee Joyner]

Love isn't all paradise

Partners don't always agree
Eye to eye, they don't see
They are sinking slowly

Just climb the ladder of love
You will find the white dove
Compromise to keep it alive
The spark that brought two people together

Remember the good times
learn from the bad
Start anew
For the love that was had

I Look at the light and see
love is an illusion to me

———————————

I started writing poetry at a young age, it became a hobby of mine
and now it's my life, I love to read and write. My inspiration is
life, my sister is my muse Allpoetry.com/Andrew_Lee

[Joanne Jin]

rain

I like to see rain

the splish splash sounds feel calming

a meditation

I diligently create and write poetry and prose, as I have a deep
passion for creative writing and aspire to see my writing
published. Additionally, I swim competitively, write and perform
spoken-word Allpoetry.com/Vintagegurl333333

[Marta E Green]

Alone In Paradise

from her vivid blue eyes
she stares at him pleading
with her arms wrapped around herself
asking for somewhere to stay
to get some warmth
temperature is below freezing

he ignores her as he crosses the street
can he hear howling in the frigid gusts of wind?
embarrassed from ignoring the coatless girl

oh, think twice, 'cause it's another day for you and me in paradise

"please help me, I'm so cold"
as rivulets of translucent water run down her cheek
limping from black tennis shoes with nary a bottom sole left

oh, think twice, 'cause it's another day for you and me in paradise*

oh God, can anything be done?
worry lines furrow her brow as her white teeth chatter
she seems used to cruelty as she rubs her bare hand under her nose
never allowed to loiter in one place for long
she tries to walk under a freeway to escape from the icy breezes

oh, think twice, 'cause it's another day for you and me in paradise

oh, think twice, it's just another day for you
you and me in paradise

Marta Green is a Texas writer. She is married, has 6 children and
4 grandchildren. She loves writing poetry, short stories and art.
Allpoetry.com/Marta_Green

Last two lines and the refrain by Phil Collins "Another Day in
Paradise"

[Tisham Dhar]

Revolutionary Philosophy

States sabotage sages
Scientists in cages
Push entrenched notions
Trigger violent emotions

Socrates drinks hemlock
Galileo in jail, heliocentric lock
Turing is chemically castrated
Bruno is burnt and staked

The power of the state
Philosophy, science abate
Religions, gods of gaps
Logic, intelligence saps

Structures bigger than us
Our life, joy and ideas sucks
Traps, games of chance, lucks
Anarchy silenced, solemn fuss

States, mega corps, tech giants, nations
Collection of individuals given body
Single cell to multicell, volvox parody
Identity subsumed
Individuality consumed
Moving to superintelligence in fractions

Like cancer 💀 philosopher removed
From the body through surgery
Brain chemistry treated in asylums
Drugs, neurotransmitter forgery
Machinery of government hums
As I, populace by propaganda moved

Colosseum, Colossus of Rhodes
Time and tide, civilization erodes
I am gone, We are still here
Perhaps immortality is near

The love of knowledge
Revolutionary philosophy
Tussle of the I vs the We
From the ego we flee
Soul searches higher
Sun, Seeker of Secrets
On cloud monkey flyer
Narratives, patterns, bets
The I is mortal
We immortal
Eternal life, final trophy 🏆
Go on! Walk off the ledge !

An invisible bridge built by We
Is really there, but I cannot see

Tisham is an Electrical and Electronics Engineer, twice failed Dr. (MBBS/PhD). He likes signal processing and generates all sorts of patterns including rhymes and poetry.
Allpoetry.com/Tisham_Dhar

[Jared Griffith]

More than the Moon loves the Stars.

The moon looks to the stars each night.
The stars look to the moon with delight.
Love between the two is forever holding tight.
Unbreakable even in the dark with no light.
It is said no greater love than this right?
That was till I met you my angel in the light.
Our love will rival this spectacle all hold so tight.
It will be said Jared loves Lisa more can it be right?
I love you more than the moon loves the stars Lisa,
because they only have the night.

Jared Griffith is from Idaho. While enjoying all the grandeur of
the West. He fills his thoughts with being the hopeless Romantic
that he is. He is so in love with Lisa Coles.
Allpoetry.com/Jared_Griffith

[Lisa F. Raines]

The Genealogist

The blood making its way
Through my blue veins today
Is full of fighters and wars
And ships and shores

I wonder at the stories
Of tattered Old Glories
On each side of every
Old memo and mem'ry

And If you find a score
Of a song not stored
You can bring it alive
With your fingers five

It's a wonder of names
From whence we came
Of documents and titles
And pictures and Bibles

But what we use next
For historical context
Is to define us by
Yesterday and why

We leave this world
With flags unfurled
For the what, who and how,
Affects more than one, now

_____

AlisRamie is from North Carolina, USA.
Interests include: philosophy, history, international relations,
poetry, art, design, jazz, funk rock, and some good old soul.
Allpoetry.com/AlisRamie

[Gary Adcock]

Freedom

as we each rise from our bed this day
we are blessed to have a choice to pray
freedom of speech, our God given right
array of stars give us peace each night

as we each rise from our bed this day
we are blessed to see our children play
safe and secure, flags fly in the breeze
oblivious as genocide happens overseas

Ukrainians rise from a shelter each day
praying their loved ones can just get away
fighting uphill battles with a will to survive
praying this be the day help will finally arrive

The devil has risen for all the world to see
greed of one-man causing millions to flee
a country being ravished, a nation in peril
soldiers storm through like animals so feral

as we each rise from our beds this day
we must get down on our knees to pray
God give them strength, let freedom prevail
send Putin back down to his eternal hell

Growing up in the Flint hills of Kansas I have always been a dreamer. I love the outdoors and good music. When you combine the two you have the makings of a great day!
Allpoetry.com/Gary_Adcock

[Keith Pailthorp]

I Drink to Forget, and It Works

at dusk reflections of regret begin to pall
lies I have lied lie far beyond recall
bells I would unring have tolled their last
folks I would unharm have long-since passed

heights I've yet to scale are now beyond the pale
depths I'll never plumb my gift to fools to come

I rest my case on this
that ignorance is bliss

and forgetting is its own path to virtue

Keith Pailthorp a retired state bureaucrat living in Davis,
California on a contrived pond and working on an unauthorized
autobiography of his checkered past.
Allpoetry.com/Keith_Pailthorp

[Alvin Chen]

A Transient Misstep

As you step downwards for the penultimate step,
It's not there.
A barely processable split second.
Why isn't there?

Your step is inevitable.
The adrenaline pumps.
You barrow downwards and pray.
You land precariously.
The ordeal is over -
your mind is tranquil again.

———————————

Alvin Chen is a poet based in New York City. Poetry is his creative medium - he enjoys writing both deep ruminations and lighthearted commentaries on the human experience.
Allpoetry.com/Alvin_Chen

[Lisa F. Raines]

Beware the "snip, snip" of Eugenics

From the decisions of the
American Supreme Court,

Fascism is making its way
into every one of our lives.

The Justices have declared
the States' sovereign control
over American bodies.

It has opened us up to the
horrors of forced pregnancies;

and, men, too, by losing
bodily autonomy,

you could be subject to the
"snip, snip" of State Eugenics!

———————

AlisRamie is from North Carolina, USA.
Interests include: philosophy, history, international relations,
poetry, art, design, jazz, funk rock, and some good old soul.
Allpoetry.com/AlisRamie

[Catherine Jean Lindsey Towery Sales]
Live Your Best Life

Life is not a do over
So be sure to live
your Best life

Life is not a commercial
Or another rerun
I'm gonna live this one
Like I nèver did before

I will Laugh and be happy,
As i live and learn
Play my favorite tune
let it play on and on

Cause I live my best life
I Love the life I live
And Live the life I love
Counting all blessings
From up up above,

Watching the sunset
Is all fun to see
singing songs I like
for all the world to see

listening to the birds
and the bees
While the wind blows

down the trees
drinking my morning coffee
as the sun Rise

Living my best life
But hating to close my eyes
This is all part of
my legacy

Reading and writing
Part of my history
No time for TV
Just my honey and me

playing with my grandchildren
Is also fun to me
Dancing in the streets
Like no one is watching me

Attending Sunday School
So I don't forget the rules
to live my best life and trying
to still be cool

———————————

Catherine Sales former Ed Counselor from Compton
CA.Catherine holds several Master's Degree in
Psychology,Education,Human Behavior,& Education Adm Cred.
Former President PA4C M.H .Advocacy 501C.
Allpoetry.com/Cathysalesmftpoet

[Mara Treviño]

Time is Nothing

Patience is a time frame-
not an emotion, but a reflection.
the notion that there is progress
even when not in motion

That's why I don't believe I can die

My epitaph will read
"Here remains a speck of dust,
the rest of me wanders"
I'll linger on everything I've ever loved
as the most imperceptible traveler

An arrow bereft in the crossfire
colliding with thunderous neutrality
and scattering like isles at sea,
the ebb and flow,
the pause in-between

I'm pretty sure I can live for always
and as long as I'm alive,
I still have time.

I'm Mara and I'm from Monterrey, México. Poetry is my very pulse and my only constant. It saved my life in more ways than I can count. Allpoetry.com/Mara_stf

[Tyrell Arnold]

Purpose of Light

We all walk through darkness

We're also bestowers of light

Our light should be used to make the journey a little less dark for our fellow man, while also freeing them of the tyranny that is their narrow evils

What other reason is there for light to exist than to reach beyond its scope

To exist where it doesn't
To shine where it hasn't shone
To peer into a gaze that antedates its blindness

————————————

Hey! Born in Atlanta! I also have web series! I just like writing poems about my feelings and whatnot, helps me cope. Allpoetry.com/Tyrell_Arnold

[Christina Marie Cuevas]

God's love is from above

◎ God's love is from above ◎

❉ How beautiful God is to shine his light on us each day.

❉ It's wonderful how God makes us his children of the world.
With our light peace and love. ❉ Striving to do good and be
good daily.

❉ God Keeps us protected and loved

❉ God teaches us to be us and different which is great God
wants us only to be our true selfs. ❉ But let his light shine
through us to all mankind.

❉ Gods love is truly from above. ❉

Love 69 - Christina Marie Cuevas, a Texas-born writer, graduated
from Everest University with a Bachelor Degree of the Paralegal
field. Currently, she is working on obtaining an MBA Degree.
Allpoetry.com/Love69

[Marie Walker]

Scars

Under your Scars , I love.

I see the Imperfections of you.

I see the love, the hate.

I see the shyness ,I see the calmness..

I see scaredness .

I see the body that is a person that ,

I enjoy.

I see your world that is alone and loneliness.

I see your heart that is torn between a heart.

I see your eyes that is hate to be a person.

I see shyness of love you have.

All I see is the reflection of me.

All you do is try, and that is what we want to see.

Love and Scaredness is put into us.

We are weak fragile humans that wants the pain to go away.

To be the beaten down when life is so small and big , at the same
time .

Even though we are not, the same person per say.

We have gone through the same thing in so much of a way.

That's what lead us to each other and have the love we didn't
have.

The Imperfections ,is all we had to love and see in each other.

We been through, all that has been thrown at us.

There could be scars on outside of us or inside of us

All, be loved and see so much of pain we been through.

Maybe that's the problem, we don't see through.
We know and see the reflection of each other.
But the love of the reflection is under the scars.
We have and we want under to see the person we are.
We might have deeper ones that ,we don't want to see.
For ourselves or each other.

I love to write Poems and just write to fulfill my mind and learn about myself. And how life is so predictable, so liveable.
Allpoetry.com/Raven_of_Night

[Perry Bach]

Seven

Seven days that you've been gone
And seven nights a silent phone
A dear john note upon my mirror
I sip another lukewarm beer
party's over

I played the part I penned our song
The words too vague I ramble on
For seven months your perfect host
I bought your time but not your soul
Tried to woo ya

Seven months of carnal nights
Now seven nights of pain and drought
My shallow words built castle walls
You longed for truth I fed you fluff
Couldn't fool ya

It felt so right now you're gone
My will now weak and you're so strong
The Blood Moon fades into the dusk
I long for dawn and crimson sun
I never knew ya

Blood N Roses I adore you
No more heartaches battle's over

Still dwelling on good times we had
Dark passion grips me once again
The seven hurts that I suppressed
While you've moved on beyond our past
I'm so blue ya

We'll meet one day and feign regrets
An awkward hug then shake his hand
I'll toss a coin to make amends
But wishing wells can't raise the dead
How'd I lose you

Blood N Roses I still adore you
Curse the heartaches battle's over

———————

Hopesummer52 is from Twin Cites MN. I form lyrics and
melodies in my head while running. Have written fifty plus
pieces since 2018. Allpoetry.com/Hopesummer52

[Angela B. Spragg]

The Beaten Child

Dusk to dawn was all hurt for me,
It was not the time for mischievous play I see,
Dusk draw nigh and so did my fate,
Hiding under the blanket to lessen her hate.

Gin and tonic mixed with hateful taste,
The beatings began as did my pain,
The night of new soreness I have found,
Nobody knows and no one around.

With the beaten body and my head,
All bloodied and, in my bed.
Beaten body I could not hide,
The bloodiness of the head slowly eating me inside.

The beaten body that should be tended with love.
Why me, I questioned the love?
Surely this madness is unfair folly?
Running away is the way for me surely.

———————————

Ms Angela Burnham Spragg is an Author from the UK, The Self-Perspective Coach and a Radio Presenter. Her poems are about the conversation with THE SELF. In the noise we forget THE SELF has a voice. Allpoetry.com/Ms._Angela_B._Spragg

[Benjamin Janke]
Marred by Memory

My world is plagued with memory
A cruel ravishing illness infecting the soil and sights I tread daily
The setting of my life abhorrently scarred with that memory,
every building I drive past marred with it like an old wound
festering with infection.
No matter how fast or how far I run it seems I cannot give my
mind respite from the haunting of those beautiful broken
memories so deeply soaked into the pores of my life. Every sign I
witness on the highway of my desperate escapes flood me with a
gut wrenching nostalgia, a once rose tinted window into the past
long since shattered, a lifetime of emotion, once my salvation now
serves as the chains that bind me and extort my pleading
confessions of love and guilt.
I can see your face in the windows of our favorite stores, I can hear
your voice like an echo trailing words we've said a thousand times.
I am haunted. I am plagued and infected just as much as the path
I tread.

Benjamin is from Moravia NY. I write poetry for many reasons
but mainly because I find the medium to be the most emotionally
expressive and I hope my writing can help show that as well
Allpoetry.com/Bensjanke

[Jennifer Grant]

Meet Me In Dreamland

I saw you in my dreams last night,
The only place we can meet in secret,
Away from prying eyes,
They wouldn't understand,
Our love is forbidden,
He takes me to the garden
Oh how the flowers grow!
Just like our desire for one another,
We spend the night in each other's embrace,
But soon I will have to go,
Dawn is breaking and my lover will fade away,
Until the next night,
When we see each other again,
In Dreamland.

———————————

Jennifer Grant is from Quincy, IL. She helps care for the elderly as a dietary aid and loves what she does. Poetry gives her an outlet to express her feelings and what's on her mind.
Allpoetry.com/Jennifer_Grant

[George L. Ellison]

A Predestined Life

My mind drifts off in reflective mood
benefitting from my solitude
a breath of wind is in the air
like a tinkling piano sound, so fair

Gone are the days now when I was young
music caressed ivory tongue
it's harder now I'm older and infirm
silken music echoes short term

I listen to echoes as they dance and play
searching my mind as they fade away
my fingers and brain aren't what they were
the time was, my reflexes were like a razor

Now, if only I could go back in time
would it now; once more reached; still be so sublime
or is our fate predestined to be
the same way each time for you and me

———————————

I have written poetry all my life but mainly since 1994, when I
really started to take it seriously
I have always enjoyed english language and literature
and generally enjoying life as I live it. Allpoetry.com/Queserasera

[Emma Steere]

Butterflies

I discovered you,
Taking glimpses at me,
Across the bar,
My heart ceased.

Your eyes,
Mysterious,
Raging inside,
Seeking to cover your pain,
The same suffering as mine.

Both our spirits are lost,
On the inside,
We are living as Robots.
Eyes filled with tears,
Never authorized,
to breathe and be me,
The same goes for you.

A few years down the line,
Again, we locked eyes,
Across the gas station parking lot.

Transformation,
New chapter,
Fresh verse,
Momentous connection.

Move forward with courage,
No fear or self-doubt,
Wake the Lion,
Road, less traveled.

Soft summer night,
You embarked on my life.
Felt from the start,
Not able to tolerate,
Being apart.

Wild sunflower,
Picked with laughter and joy.
Beneath the twilight.
This depicted,
The beginning,
Of our life.

Brushed your body,
Couldn't wait til' later,
Steal a kiss,
Behind the car.

Best,
Forever remembered.
Swept me off my feet,
Time stands still,
Gratified.

I never kissed a mug,
With zest, like yours,
Soul fire.

Inner voice,
Said slow down.
Risk that was needed,
To not fall apart.
Shove that pain,
Deep down.

Exposed and Revealed,
Dive in,
Sunshine glimmer,
My heart is yours.
Stay up and talk,
Dusk till Dawn.

This could be our last, first kiss,
Executed carefully.
Final time,
Offering our hearts,
To another.

Deep breath,
Shiver.
Goosebumps all over.

No symphony,
But you'll know it,
I guarantee,
Twitter Pated feeling,
Butterflies.

With the right person,
Think about your feeling,
Security.

Out here in the wild,
Weeds all around,
In a rush,
Just the breeze and owls,
Lips on yours,
I knew,
This had to be love.
Butterflies.

Afraid to fall,
Gazing at you,
Skeptics abruptly went away.
Breaking my codes,
Before learning your all.

Later, looking back,
Our prior pain,
Departing,
Soon to be invisible.

Love isn't random,
We're chosen,
And I can only imagine,
Our vibing state of mind,
Even when it's pouring down.

Every heart has a rhythm,
Let yours beat loudly,
For all to hear.
Don't fear doing something different,
Dare to be something more.

You're the only one of you,
You're something else,
Everything I need.
I know we just met,
You got my hopes up.

Close your eyes,
Explain your dreams.
Never could I imagine,
You and me,
In this moment.
I'm right where I want to be.

Kiss me in the dark,
Turn out the noise,
Until we see sparks.
Your soul a magnet,
Attracting mine, to you,
Like a fairytale.

Your strength,
The drumming of your heart,
Puts me at ease.

Went heart first.
Could be forever,
Knowing, I might get hurt.

I need you,
Memories continue,
Hopeless romantic.

Head over heels,
Butterflies 🦋

Tipsy,
Can't stop kissing,
Forever, here we come.
Said the words,
No doubt in my mind,
"I love you",
Your reply,
"Thank you".

Dizziness overcame me,
Gentleman, you are,
Took me inside.

Next day,
I Recreated,
Wanting to blossom and bloom,
Growing together,
Thankfully,
This time,
You reciprocated.
Wanting to water our garden,
And stay fueled to keep going.

Giving all of you,
Risking it all,
Though it's hard.
Hearts showing,
You're too good to be true.

Be my man,
Hold my hand.
Wrapped around your finger,
Against all odds,
Climb to the top,
Move in harmony.

I know we will be alright,
Clouds formed as hands,
You're my shelter.
True love,
Best friends,
Trust,
The Angels sing.

Take your last name,
Put it where my name is.
Drive the doubt away,
I promise till the end,
I'll never run,
I'll give you love.

Church bells ring,
Kissing under the moon,
Love on the brain,
Butterflies.

Kisses and hugs,
My love is endless.
Happiness,
True and authentic,
Weak in the knees.

There is nothing better,
Then you and me,
together.

Stuck on you,
The bliss of your hand,
Cradling mine.
Heart fluttering,
On cloud nine.
Possess my heart,
Truly meant to be.

No soul, knows me better,
Don't have to play a part,
You Make me feel bliss,
You and I could change the game.

Struggle is seen.
Patience,
See it through.
It's Me and You.

I'll show you love,
Even if I nag you in the morning,
night,
And all twenty- four hours of life.

Your brown eyes,
All tangled up.
Even if the sky is falling down,
Let it go.

One of those weeks,
Stuck on repeat.
Too much on my plate,
We've paid our dues,
I know,
I can be wrapped up,
You are who keeps me on the ground.

The here and now.
The world is a lost and found,
It could try and take us,
But victory is contagious.
Together,
We'll always win.

You provide,
What I need,
My heart is full.
Commemorate,
Celebrate.

The reason I love you,
Is you,
Being you,
And all we've been through.
Butterflies.

Renowned chaos coordinator. Mom of 4, step mom of 3. Past
Trauma. Attending college and General Manager of an outdoor
Whitewater/ Fly Fishing company.
Allpoetry.com/Chaos_Coordinator

[Lisa F. Raines]

Dollars and Sense

My, my, my, brother,
you may win when you gamble,
but you don't care about any other.

You use people in your life —
making us all into fools —
even your father and mother.

You certainly will lose
when you lie and choose
to obfuscate and cover.

Get wise, young man,
you will lose more than dollars
if you have no sense to recover.

———————————

AlisRamie is from North Carolina, USA.
Interests include: philosophy, history, international relations,
poetry, art, design, jazz, funk rock, and some good old soul.
Allpoetry.com/AlisRamie

[Alwyn Barddylbach]

Fly Against The Wind With Me

If you can spare thirteen minutes of your day
for sake of the next three years and well beyond;
If you're undecided, choked numb by smoke and mirrors
or with a moment's hesitation have your say;
If you're not quite sure the whims and moods of this
land, who would take your money, shake your hand,
pretend to care, lie, cheat and lose their way;
If you're angry still, standing after bushfire, flood and
virus, doubt or wonder who shall lead us
beyond this crucial merry-go-round of May; and
if you want the best for your country, your children,
not the worst we've seen in bogan disarray -
Then yours is a future worthy for the taking.

Let's fly against the wind together; now my friend
you're ready to cast that vital vote today.

_____

'If you can fill the unforgiving minute with sixty seconds worth of
distance run, yours is the earth and everything that's in it' (RK
1895). On the eve of an Australian Federal election (2022).
Allpoetry.com/Barddylbach

[April Hamlin-Sache]

My Strength

I have something to be grateful for,
I have something to smile about.
It is you, my strength,
my resilience.

I flow with the rhythm,
like the ocean waves,
back and forth,
a lot of my days.

Just because I am free from captivity,
does not mean that things do not bother me,
paranoia haunts me.

I am full of screams within,
at times I release them.

I paid my dues,
I am thankful for the credit that I have received.

As long as I breathe
my strength will never leave me,
because I will put up a fight to hold on tight to it.

It is you, my strength
that allows me to keep living,
a higher power within me that breathes oxygen daily.

Congratulations to myself,
I am not only a woman with resilience,
I am a lady full of my strength.

I am originally from Indiana. I have 5 poetry books, 2 books of
short stories and 7 series on amazon.com. I am a PT receptionist
and a writer. I love what I do! I Luv reading poetry!
Allpoetry.com/April_Sache

[Tim Cedillo Jr]

Tears of pain

The sky opens up,
It screams out in pain.
Lightening streaks and thunder crashes.
As it cries tears of rain.
Clouds so gloomy they hide the sun.
The day is looking dark.
The tear drops splash against the flowers.
Not knowing their important part.
As the sky cries further,
The teardrops land and flood the ground.
The grass grows greener,
And the flowers bud.
With the new life these tears have found.
And as the storm rolls away,
The sun comes out,
and dries the floods of tears
It's strange a little pain,
Can make things grow for years.
But amongst all things,
The show of strength.
That comes from all the tears.

———————————

From Williamsburg, Ky. Tim has used poetry to help him
overcome addiction, and the problems that come along with it.
He has came a long way in his recovery proving words truly are
powerful. Allpoetry.com/Tim_Cedillo_Jr.

[Stephen Puls]

Daddy is Lost

Dear son,

Have been shipwrecked on this island
There's no way I'm getting home
Without a way to contact you
The ocean ate my phone
So I'm writing you this letter
Your Dad misses your smile
I won't forget our long walks
Where you would talk all the while
I'm staring at the sun going down
I'm torn to pieces without you
Of all the things I miss the most
It's everything you do
I need you to be a gentleman
Be kind to your future wife
Dad can't see you graduate
Or help you with your life
Remember me like I will you
Don't forget daddy's face
Try to imagine if you can
Daddy flew to outer space
I will never get to hold you
Or look into your blue eyes
Never get to tell you stories
Or hear your cute goodbyes

Never get to see you grow
Or earn your first big raise
Never get to see you marry
Then give you your big praise
I'm sorry son I'm leaving you
I never wanted it this way
I'm never getting back to you
No matter if I pray
Tell your mother that I loved her
She was my wonderful
You, my son were the perfect son
You made me colorful
Be strong, honest and true
From a boy become a man
Daddy will keep you in view
Grow up a gentleman
Goodbye it's not forever
Keep me inside your heart
Someday we will be together
Even after I depart

Love,
Daddy

————————————

My writing is my therapy. I was an E.M.T. For many years and
have some anxiety type issues. Poetry gives my mind peace. I am
from Tewksbury, Ma. Allpoetry.com/Stephen2

[Shari Madison]

Shades of yesterday

Today is a sunny day. I sit quiet in my space wasting the time away.

The light comes in through the window casting a shade upon the room - takes me back to a time when my heart would swoon.
Waiting for you to walk through the door with that smile on your face - Oh how this shade takes me back to that place.
It was a season of love, laughter and something new. Now I sit holding my heart feeling so blue.
My eyes are locked on that clock on the wall counting the minutes going by as the shade begins to fall.
A feeling of relief as the sun moves around. The memories begin to fade along with the fleeing shade about to hit the ground.
It's time to put my feet back on the floor and remind my heart that, that was then and this is now. Nothing more.
miles apart...

———————

I love hard and give all I'm capable of in the moment. I struggle with letting love in and it pushing people away. So I write about the aftermath. Heartbreak at my own hand.
Allpoetry.com/Shari_Madison

[Kh ventura]

Dreaming

Swallow me up and let the
universe consume me.
My body is now a demon
playground, can anyone hear me?
I'm here, yet nowhere to be found
I'm all out of words,
I screamed and screamed
my voice echoes through
this cave of darkness

You are quick to fade in and out
nor a raven's feather or a spray
of your cologne can summon you.
If I lay here awake.
My essence becomes
shaken with destruction
My hands melt into the bed,
as I try to pull you out
I try to abduct you
falling asleep is
the only way to see you
I'll take it, I'll travel and travel
until I die here forsaken

Kh ventura is from Maryland
She loves writing and sees it as a way of expression, and healing
my ultimate goal is to be the voice of those who are afraid to
speak. Allpoetry.com/Kh_Ventura

[Sandy Bair]

My Sunflower

Your memory is embroidered in my heart
burning brightly
from within
flowing outward
to light my path

Beautifully engraved
upon the canvas
of my life
words of deepest, honeyed affection
you spoke grow as wild
as the sunflowers covering
Texas fields

I recall times when you held me on your lap
and brushed the dirt right off my knee;
or just held me
cushioned to your bosom
and
times of holding your hands
all these are precious thoughts to me...
engraved forever
in my memory

The day my Sunflower
withered
arrived too soon;

jarring my spirit...
cutting and biting

So difficult
for me to understand and accept
you needed to
be at peace; body, mind, and soul

God only chooses the prettiest flowers for his Heavenly bouquet

All the arrangements were taken care of...
the flowers, the music; the service
Pastor Shelley delivered the eulogy
as I sat with my broken heart
dripping down my face

I often sit and gaze
at your photograph
just to get through each passing day
and when I spot the occasional
sunflower, I smile through
glass tears
knowing you're still watching
over me

My Mother; my Sunflower

––––––––––––––––

Heavenly Angel has been writing poems and stories since she was
a little girl. Creativity is her lifeblood.
Allpoetry.com/Heavenly_Angel

[Elizabeth Sacco]

Resemblance

Six foot three
And all I see
Is a man resembling my brother

He died in September
And I still remember
The shaken face of my mother

Eleven years after
I'm ashamed of my laughter
Telling jokes on Christmas day

Taken back to the past
My heart beating fast
I wish that he chose to stay

Goosebumps on my skin
Tear stains on my chin
I still can't believe that it's true

The nights are long
And I don't feel strong
I see him in all that you do

Surrounded by lies
The tears in my eyes
And answers I will never know

My biggest confession
Is I'll always question
Why did he decide to let go?

I hate suicide
I hate that he died
I hate that I feel so alone

The thoughts in my head
Turn to nightmares instead
I look like flesh ripped from a bone

Why is it you?
I just wish that I knew
How one person can seem like another

The comfort I seek
I feel when you speak
You remind me so much
Of my brother

———————————

Elizabeth is from Boston, Massachusetts. She has a passion for film, theater, art, and storytelling. Allpoetry.com/Elizardbreath

[Rhonda Ramsey Cash]

By Best Friend

Lord, breathe on me bring
heaven down with a smile
let me give You a kiss
and lean on You for a while.

Teach me Your wisdom
how to love and to care
letting me know that You
will always be there.

The fragrance of Your Spirit
is sweet to carry me through
the long year's mile.
giving me strength to persue.

A friendship to last eternal
as we walk each day
giving me Your love
and a reason to be saved.

I am a Christian poet who has been writing since 1990 and have
deep spiritual beliefs God has given me
a talent of poetry and I am to share it with a lost and dying world.
Allpoetry.com/Godspoetwriter4

[Bobbie Breden]

So Deep in the Midnight Hour

So deep in the midnight hour
In an ether of indigo dye
Trees stand like shadowy towers
Moon's face crossed by clouds on the fly

Your image descending the stair way
Caught from the corner of my sight
Your likeness, transparent and deep gray
Your figure would never alight

Your appearance was gone, leaving no trace
My perceptions record disbelief
Your ashes reposed on the bookcase
The urn, marked with tears from my grief

Now, your essence guards over my heart here
The strength of your love had such power
Your visit brought comfort, not fear, dear
So deep in the midnight hour

———————————

Retired Lady Leatherneck (US Marine), Renaissance woman, and a lover of life's mysteries. I'm interested in how others view the universe, and welcome opportunities to see it through their eyes. Allpoetry.com/Captain_B2

[Patricia Marie Batteate]

The Cycle of Life

When we're born
We wonder
As tots
We explore
As children
We wish
As teens
We want more
As students
We learn
As adults
We earn
As parents
We hope
As grandparents
We cope
As elders
We pray
For one more day
To wonder...

───────────────

I am a 7th generation Californian. I am an engineer, poet and artist. 'Tolerance is a gauge used to determine just how much a person is willing to put up with' Allpoetry.com/Patricia_Marie

Walking With My Destiny

Walking on life's pathway
one day I sense a presence near
matching my swing and sway
and suddenly I know no fear.

Don't go, don't go,
stay a while
you make me know,
you make me smile

Shadows scatter with every stride
your light is glowing more and more
like you were always by my side
sun is shining from my core

Don't go, don't go,
stay a while
you make me glow,
you make me smile

I want you to have a song
as all love aspirations do
it will say we belong
so walk with me, I'll walk with you

Don't go, don't go
stay a while
you make me flow
you make me smile

Through our life's highs and lows
together we will share each day.
What will be, no one knows
walk with me we'll be okay.

Don't go, don't go
stay a while
you make me grow
you make me smile

now advancing the twilight
yet still you radiate for me
even nearing the longest night
I'm walking with my destiny

Walking with my destiny

Don't go, don't go,
just rest a while
I want you to know,
you always made me smile.

————————————

Not a wordsmith just an ordinary joe, see a reason and rhymes
seem to flow. Such things Larcs couldn't see, until lockdown
2020. Love living, live loving is his call, and being kind to ONE
and ALL Allpoetry.com/Lockdown_Larcs

[Kenny Charnell]

Trudge On Into Weariness

Trudge on into weariness,
you've earned yourself some sleep.
Your shoulders stoop,
your gait is slow,
your daily industry is complete.

Tonight, please take to resting.
Your responsibilities have been met.
Those that count on you for provision,
have not been found wanting.
You strive for them without regret.

Tomorrow will bring new opportunity.
At its beginning your step will spring.
You will be happy in the challenges.
And if work itself was musical
your labors could not help but sing.

Such is the price of dependability.
Accountability is the coin you pay.
Children fed. Spouse sustained.
Satisfaction in your respectability.
Would you have it any other way?

I am a husband, father, grandpa, son, brother, deacon
(Presbyterian), and recently a retiree. I'm trying to figure out what
retiree means to me. Poetry, I'm sure will be a part of it.
Allpoetry.com/Arlboy

[David Newton]

A Sacrifice of Knowing

A nervous heart pounds
from desire acknowledged
by a muse long thought lost.

Soul set on fire
by an act of devotion,
intimately embracing from afar.

Mind sent racing
into peaceful repose
after willing unwitting recruited.

Longing never absent
rediscovered uncovered,
by just a touch.

Physical concession
gives mental release
to an old troubled mind.

Years rewind in seconds,
and lovers reintroduced.
A sacrifice of knowing.

———————————

Poetry allows me to express difficult thoughts and feelings. There
is a story behind everything I write. Each poem lets me clearly
remember something, without revealing everything to the reader.
Allpoetry.com/David_Newton

[Douglas Smith]

A Night Turned Sideways

The countertop clinks after each shot being taken,
The reveling and drinking making joy unmistaken.
Competing in seeking each other's validation,
But leaving is needed to assure tomorrows vocation.

Submitting to the back seat of the call for assisting.
Resisting the tempting of leaning and sleeping.
Stopping and accelerating and turning to reach the destination.
Stationed at a red light, staring outside and waiting.
Hearing shattering, crashing, crumpling, and screaming.

Looking forward pejoratively before realizing the horror,
The car in our corridor smoking more and more.
My door swings forward as I charge toward pure misfortune.
Emotions delete, like a story with no orator.

Airbags deployed, the only one in says she's okay.
Then I look away and see the other against a wall splayed.
The legs move again without further delay,
A race to see the state of someone's worst day.

All the windows are shattered from the occurred disaster,
Looking inside, two young girls, faces bloodily plastered.
The driver crying, describing suffering that just happened.
Circumventing the crash to help out the lucky passenger first.

Then a sight that'd instill fright as black as the night.
Another plight hiding behind the first cry.
Head laying awry, unable to see eyes.
Crimson face contrasting an attire so bright.

Breaking the seat to reach this last casualty,
Crawling in, unfastening, then hearing things unsettling.
A door swings, an exclaim stating impending doom rising.
The ride is catching fire, igniting urgency unappetizing.

Adrenaline surges, purges inability to lift.
Yanking, grabbing, pulling, anything to get us out of this shit.
The sounds of her shoes as i withdrew from the accident,
Dragging, scraping, ingraining from the action.

Gently propping her body on a wall,
Incessantly cropping my thoughts to deal with it all.
Allowing mental corralling, ensuring her existence remains
continual.
The visual is residual.
The sensation, invocation, nothing negating wherewithal to care
for her.

Before I knew, my hoodie is removed.
Pressing through and removing blood accrued.
Eyes meet, I can see her view is askew.
One eye denied sight with what I'm trying to do.

Robotic reactions become automatic,
This unique moment indescribably tragic.

The white hoodie consumed with red from what just happened.
An unnatural faction of something so disastrous.

The concern of preserving human life
The yearn to make learned her human right
The feeling of her breathing becoming light
The desiring of needing to make her confident, non-contrite.

Minutes escaped, it's removed from my face
This moment between us lost in time and space
Despite that, to this day I can still picture the place
A way for fate to say we're both destined to cross ways.

The moment of feeling the tapping on my shoulder
Seeing help has arrived and not denying better fortune
The assuring reminding that home is towards us.
Engorging thus, destroying tormenting thoughts.

My family is full of law enforcement and military. A legacy of
heroism. I was never given the chance to prove to myself I have
the drive to run towards the fire, until this night.
Allpoetry.com/Djgs117

[Douglas Smith]

The Bird

A red sky flies high ringing in the night,
Crimson grass painted from the perished of the fight.
The war is won, my banners are flying high,
But the message must be delivered before the first light.
With the bird in the air, the march back is the last to despair.

Walls rise in the horizon as home is now sighted.
Only thing on my mind is the smell of the trees, the taste of the
mead, and my Queen at my side.
The gates open, the smallfolks cheer, and the horses rear.
Shoutings of "Long live the King!" bringing home ever near,
Drowning out memories of battle which brought any fear.
The leers and jeers erased by cheers and peers,
It's time to feast and put down the spears.

Cups are being poured as armor gets relieved.
Approaching the head seat, I'm greeted by the embrace of my
Queen.
She's the reason I fight, my desire to reign
All the blood shed to ensure her hearts beating,
"Let us drink and eat to celebrate His victory!" she screams.
As the bird flies ever forward, soaring towards destiny.

Jesters are jesting, singers are singing,
Flagons are cheersing, lutes are ringing.
Course after course the cooks keep bringing,

Cup after cup we all keep downing.
Deep into the night reveling in the festivities.
Is this the fifth cup? The sixth cup? Or the nineteenth?
"The final course I will now serve!"
Yells the Queen from my right-hand seat,
"And let this be a lesson to those with thoughts of usurp!"

Returning from the kitchen with a single silver platter,
With a cover engraved of our love story and laughter.
In front of me its placed with a smile across Her face.
Through the hall they all stare irate.
I lift up the cover, a bleeding heart awaits.
Confusion and delusion fill my brain,
Looking back up at my Queen, the Reaper has taken her place.
The subjects start shouting "All hail his Disgrace!"
Then the pain hits like a war drums bass.
I look down at my chest, blood dripping through empty space.
Falling forward like I've been struck by a mace.

The bird enters from an open balcony,
Accompanying the sun's morning beam.
Lands on my plate, blood and wine at its feet.
"The enemy is inside the gates."
The message is finally received.

———————————

I am trusting, ever loving, to the point of blindness. Might be a
crime thus, mindless love until you find one that reminds us you
deserve more. Much. A reminding crux, you're entitled to such.
Allpoetry.com/Djgs117

[Vicki Moore]

I Come From..

I come from the city
catching fireflies
playing hopscotch
and badminton
with my family
dinner at 6:30
summers riding bikes
coming home with the streetlights
walking around
and climbing trees
in an innocent time

I come from being raped
at the age of thirteen
on my very first date
being called a whore
by him and more
being told no good boy
would take me out now
they could all tell
I wasn't a virgin
and that all boys wanted
was sex

I come from drinking
at school to avoid

my own thoughts
and using drugs
to hide my pain
and I never told anyone
about what happened
I didn't even have the words
to know myself what happened

I come from marrying a man
who was not very nice
though he said it was love
I didn't know the difference
thought name calling and hitting
were the way couples acted
since I knew no better
I still felt like a whore

I come from having two beautiful sons
and leaving their father
time after time
going back to him
because I didn't
know anything else
finally I left him
to stay in a shelter
hiding from him
because my children
and the memories
of my family and childhood
taught me about love

I come from going to college
at the age of forty something
and finding a man
who was gentle and kind
who encouraged my art
my work
and my education
and most importantly
gave me a backbone
so I could build boundaries

I come from loving myself
for who I am
and all these things that
I come from

_____

I am a 60 year old woman learning to express myself with poetry.
I started writing in High School but stopped for many years. I
have survived many things but I have never given up hope.
Allpoetry.com/Vicki_moore

[Ben Pickard]

A Grievance Against The Trees

Each time the leaves vacate their em'rald perch,
A grief in me begins to twist and burn.
Perhaps, to them, an em'rald has no worth,
And so they fall and so I grieve and yearn.
The summer sun burns dimmer than before
So never tricks my heart or tempts my mind;
This battle has become a yearly war,
But golden rays no longer leave me blind.
In time, my feet make paths through all that's been -
The rustle racks my soul and breaks my bones.
To think I walk on waste that once was green,
And sing the fall in perfect monotone.
Each year, you dress your limbs and tease us all,
But hark! I hear the winter's blasted call.

_____

English sonnet . Married father of four, I live in the UK and love reading and writing poetry. My other hobbies include reading the classics, walking and watching films. Allpoetry.com/Ben_Pickard

[Larry Wells Jr]

This Paper Heart

I hold here a replica
A model of my own heart
At times it is hard to tell which is real
This heart made of paper
Or the one of flesh and blood

While that may sound odd
It's true that this origami heart
Cannot stand against the current of a river
The heart in my chest
Cannot hold its own when held before you

I didn't know it would be you
That the distance I chose would eviscerate
So it was distance like scissors tore
Paper and flesh alike
Each a reflection of the other

This life without you is much akin to death
The pale rictus of the beyond
Etched onto my own face
A pain more permanent as if carved in stone
And not this flimsy heart of cardboard paper

Yet that being said it's you
That tethers me to this earth
Keeping myself and this material heart

Here away from a new beginning
The start of a transcendental journey

The intricate lines across this heart of mine
Form tessellations for all to see
An art as unique as my own poetry
Of which all you've inspired
Everything laid bare on the page I hold here

For you I'm esurient
Craving, hungering for that I don't need
Gripping tightly to an idea
A hope and a dream
That has never shown signs of fruition

But now the stage is set
The fans want to see an apogee
One final climactic scene
The want me to release you
Like a wild hawk once injured

Yet that's something I could never bare
To watch you soar on the wind
Towards the cumulus clouds
That I might never again lay eyes upon
So I give you that paper heart that I here hold

Larry Wells Jr is 19 years old, and has lived all across the United States. In that time he has found solace in books and in writing, it has helped him cope with his 2 medical discharges from the Army
Allpoetry.com/FallinInTheWells

[Douglas Smith]

"My" Pride

The cold on your face
Countertop conveys
Mind going between things

Like your legs

In a dream state
Feel my needing
Through it, turning head, "Please."

You know it's right
Scrying into the night
I'm only here because of your stride.

My heart bleeds for thee

I crave you always
I stay watching hallways
I want you to shine bright

At the same time
Your want, a sunrise
Encumbered, our throats prying

No need to breathe

Deny if you will
But you won't
Not a drill

I am yours
You are mine
This time, former ceases

At least, yet

Us is scattered
Outclassed rapture
Breathtaking atmosphere

Asking more

Wanting what's in store
No more
Releasing control

Oh, more

You know you belong
To my whims, beautiful sin
But worship my govern

You know
Also
The book will flip script

Reach the line, "finished"

Unleash you
And me
Rabid curs

Sleeping tigers
Responding
No one unnerved

A zoo with no preserves

Now the lion
Himself, beside
Processing his Pride

Yours

———————————

I am trusting, ever loving, to the point of blindness. Might be a
crime thus, mindless love until you find one that reminds us you
deserve more. Much. A reminding crux, you're entitled to such.
Allpoetry.com/Djgs117

[Jared Griffith]

My Lisa

A woman of the people the claim has been made.

A champion for the innocent who fought hard every day.

True to herself integrity's right hand you could say.

She is the one I love even to her dismay.

She is humble and doesn't see the mountains she has moved away.

A titan of a person whose wisdom and determination could stop the oceans waves.

A fierce champion, a tender lover a role model to all on full display.

I hope and dream to marry her one magnificent day.

Lisa coles you should be proud and stand tall, this world is better with you leading the way.

Jared Griffith is from Idaho. While enjoying all the grandeur of the West. He fills his thoughts with being the hopeless Romantic that he is. Allpoetry.com/Jared_Griffith

[Tim Cedillo Jr]

The Ringer

I'm not content till I'm almost dead.
I get so messed up I can't hold up my head.
It always ends in immoral doom.
As my high crashes the world turns gloom.
Another fix for me to consume.
Another spiritual death,
Puts my soul in a tomb.
Entrapped its a slave I'm better off dead.
The unseen evil in control of my head.

I'd do what I must to seek total control.
But it's not me driving down the dark road.
Just an empty shell with no lights.
My eyes would turn cold,
And black as the night.
Affixated on the goal to get myself right.
A needle in my arm was the ultimate high.

I was ran through the ringer,
My own private hell.
Disgusted with life I thought I had failed.
Not knowing the lessons,
I had learned in that time.
The strength and the courage,
I would gain out of life.

The will to keep going no matter the road.
Or the impact on people when my story is told.

We all have problems accepting our past.
We all always struggle,
trying to get things back.
None of us are ever,
where we think we should be.
Your all just as insecure as me.
But success isn't measured by all that you gain.
It's getting up and keep going
no matter the pain.

———————

From Williamsburg, Ky. Tim has used poetry to help him overcome addiction, and the problems that come along with it. He has come a long way in his recovery proving words truly are powerful. Allpoetry.com/Tim_Cedillo_Jr.

[Joshua Aaron Lowe]

We Met In a Dream Once

My heart beats faster, exposed to the cold
Gleaming violently and silently in the dim yellow light
Vision blurs with the anticipation as we give new to the old
Smile ever turning, yet my mind remains still

You just stood there

Raise my hand, but it stays by my side
Tongue hidden behind bated breath, I stare
Moving closer, am I to you or you to me
I can't decide
Mind is turning, stomach-churning
Your skin is so fair

You never said a word
Until you did, my ears ringing with silence

Still, your words caress and shape my being
Though your hand never reaches for me
Your fingerprints remain
Impressions on my skin, heart left beating but feeling as though
it's fleeing

You turned and walked away

Relief and fear fill my senses, anxiously anticipating
Painful tears stream down my face, unsure if from fear or joy
Some say love can be abrasive to the soul
The thought comforted

The implication devastating
Familiarity can feel like coming home
But what is home when it's full of drunken lies

I stood in the room alone

Contemplating life in all its tedious expressions
Hating to be without, fearful to be forgot
Holding tight to toxic transgressions
This sadness is accustomed, forgoing the help I sought

I lie awake and just stare

Stare into the ceiling above
Engulfing textured paint above
Leaving nothing for the eye to see
Yet the memory remains.

Coexisting with the present
Duality overshadowing
Persistence met with an unmovable feeling
Rooting itself within the confines of the mind
Entangling the very thought of progression
Suppressing it until there is no more

We met in a dream once
But you never left:

_____

Josh is a Marine Corps. and Army combat veteran with a Master's
in Professional Writing. Poetry serves as his emotional outlet
between being a human rights advocate and a nonprofit program
manager. Allpoetry.com/Joshua_Lowe

[S. Libellule]

I Am Because We Are

So much of each day
is spent the same way
looking out beyond the horizon
looking inward to secrets held

With all we have dared
all that we shared
you do know me
better than I know myself

Through pleasure and pain
sunshine and rain
we have stayed right here
together

Though the days ahead
may have their share of dread
I know I am strong
when you hold my hand

No matter what I face
I treasure this special place
whether you are near or far

I am because we are

Originally from New England, Libellule currently lives outside of Birmingham, Alabama. Poetic influences include Mary Oliver, Billy Collins and ee cummings. Allpoetry.com/Little_Dragonfly

[Jennifer Olson]

Chaos

When the chaos settles
and I look to my side
Will you still be reaching for me,
or long gone in a distant stride?

Created the.stoned.pen on instagram as an outlet for my thoughts
through the turmoil of life. The initial poems were written while
being medicated, however I find I am writing poems daily now.
Allpoetry.com/Dwolson2

[Catherine Jean Lindsey Towery Sales]

The Bible

Basic Instructions Before
Leaving 🌍 Earth
That's the book 📚
For me in the
Beginning was
The word and the
World was
with thee

The Bible

It's the good news
The gospel
I Spread
All over the land
And sea
North East West
And South
The word will
Always be
with thee

The Bible

Inspired by God
Given to 👦 man
Read it every day
To be bless

In so many ways
believe in eternity
I believe in thee
I believe in God
I believe in the
Trinity
I believe in
Everlasting life
Its free if
You believe in
The Father and the
Son you will have
an everlasting life

The Bible

John three sixteen
Tells both you and me
For God so loved
The 🌍 world
That he gave his
Only begotten Son
that whosoever
Believeth in thee
shallNot perish
butHave an
everlasting Life
I believe in the
Father and the son
Have an everlasting
Life John 3:16

I believe in the
Holy Trinity
The Father,Son and
The Holy Spirit
Have an everlasting
Life

The Bible

Is the word
The word was
with Thee
the Word dwells
In me
The word is
The trinity
The word
Is all three
The Father,son
And the
Holy Spirit
Dwells in all
Three
Called the Trinity

The Bible

Catherine Sales former Ed Counselor from Compton
CA.Catherine holds several Master's Degree in
Psychology,Education,Human Behavior,& Education Adm Cred.
Former President PA4C M.H .Advocacy 501C.
Allpoetry.com/Cathysalesmftpoet

[Samuel K. Williams III MD CPG]

Love Fried Hard

Love, I thought I knew
Small, pretty, soft toes
Can I paint them pink?
Soft, pretty, brown hands
Can I paint them too?
Full, luscious, pink lips
Can I kiss them dear?
Lipstick or chapstick
Softest kiss I imagine
I hate love, I love love
I'm so confused
Born with it
Maybelline ain't it
A beauty so rare
Short hair, long hair both
Make me smile
Frown at me, smile at me, just look at me
My heart, your heart
Two hearts, can be one heart
Will they meet again?
Love is never easy
My girl, your world
I'll have my love fried hard, with you

41 year old physician and father of 3 children living in Albany, Georgia. I currently practice tele-health and plan on publishing my entire poetry collection within a year.
Allpoetry.com/The_Thoughtsider

[Douglas Smith]

Fighting Me

The bottle

A throttle

Herd of cattle

Colossal

False apostle

Hollow coddle

Encoding capture

Rapture

Intact

But unwrapped

Ignoring

Destroying

Hoping

Crowning

King Louis

XVI

Intrigued

fatigued

repeat

Future

Foreseen

Incomplete

Obsolete

The creep

Retreat

Bleak
A leak
Incomplete
Street
A shriek
Discrete
Unneeded
Wishing
It's seen

I am trusting, ever loving, to the point of blindness. Might be a crime thus, mindless love until you find one that reminds us you deserve more. Much. A reminding crux, you're entitled to such.
Allpoetry.com/Djgs117

[Patricia Marie Batteate]

Time May Heal But it Doesn't Forget

Don't make me regret
My apology in this case
It's not about pride
Or the saving of face

It's about my conscience
And making things right
Why must everything
Turn into a fight

You know how I loathe
Yelling and screaming
I ask myself, honestly
Is this love worth redeeming

It's tolerance that determines
How much I can take
It's forgiveness that allows
A truce for us to make

We all have done things
Of which we have regrets
Forgiveness doesn't erase
Those things we can't forget

I am a 7th generation Californian. I am an engineer, poet and artist. 'Tolerance is a gauge used to determine just how much a person is willing to put up with.' Allpoetry.com/Patricia_Marie

Printed in Great Britain
by Amazon